The Special Education Toolbox

The Special Education Toolbox

Supporting Exceptional Teachers, Students, and Families

Nicholas D. Young, Melissa A. Mumby, and Michaela F. Rice

ROWMAN & LITTLEFIELD
Lanham • Boulder • New York • London

Published by Rowman & Littlefield
An imprint of The Rowman & Littlefield Publishing Group, Inc.
4501 Forbes Boulevard, Suite 200, Lanham, Maryland 20706
www.rowman.com

6 Tinworth Street, London SE11 5AL

Copyright © 2019 by Nicholas D. Young, Melissa A. Mumby, and Michaela F. Rice

All rights reserved. No part of this book may be reproduced in any form or by any electronic or mechanical means, including information storage and retrieval systems, without written permission from the publisher, except by a reviewer who may quote passages in a review.

British Library Cataloguing in Publication Information Available

Library of Congress Cataloging-in-Publication Data

Names: Young, Nicholas D., 1967- author. | Mumby, Melissa A., 1977- author. | Rice, Michaela, author.
Title: The special education toolbox : supporting exceptional teachers, students, and families / by Nicholas D. Young, Melissa A. Mumby and Michaela Rice.
Description: Lanham : Rowman & Littlefield, [2019] | Includes bibliographical references.
Identifiers: LCCN 2019000815 (print) | LCCN 2019008267 (ebook) | ISBN 9781475847970 (electronic) | ISBN 9781475847956 (cloth) | ISBN 9781475847963 (pbk.) Subjects: LCSH: Special education—United States—Handbooks, manuals, etc.
Classification: LCC LC3981 (ebook) | LCC LC3981 .Y684 2019 (print) | DDC 371.9—dc23
LC record available at https://lccn.loc.gov/2019000815

Contents

Preface vii

Acknowledgments ix

1 The Fundamentals of Special Education: Defining Disabilities and the Federal Laws that Provide Guidance 1

2 Response to Intervention and Multi-Tiered Systems of Support: A Close Examination of the Prereferral Process 19

3 Determining the Need for Special Education Services: A Spotlight on the Assessment and Diagnostic Process 29

4 Laying the Foundation for Success: Developing Meaningful Individualized Education Plans 39

5 Finding the Right Fit: The Least Restrictive Environment 49

6 Understanding the Role of the Paraprofessional: Leveraging Student Success 61

7 It's Not All About Academics: Addressing Disability-Related Behavior Problems and Social Deficits 71

8 Expanding the Team: Effective Collaboration with Outside Services and Professionals 81

9 Harnessing the Home-School Connections: Planning for Effective Parent-Teacher Partnerships 89

10 Transition Planning: Ensuring Successful Post-Secondary Outcomes for Students with Disabilities 99

11 Resources to Support Special Education Professionals 107

References 113
About the Authors 127

Preface

The Special Education Toolbox: Supporting Exceptional Teachers, Students, and Families was written for school administrators; policymakers; pre-service, novice, and seasoned teachers; paraprofessionals; school psychologists and related service providers; and the families of children who may be entering the special education arena or who have been previously identified with one of the predetermined disabilities as explained by the federal Individuals with Disabilities Education Act (IDEA) (Center for Parent Information & Resources, 2017a). Navigating the world of special education can be both challenging and fulfilling. As disability diagnoses have increased substantially over the past decade, having a solid understanding of the practices, procedures, and legalities surrounding special education services has become increasingly necessary to ensure the success of this population of students and those who are dedicated to working with or on their behalf.

This book aims to provide practical information for both current and aspiring special education teachers, special education related professionals, parents, school administrators and policymakers on topics that are most relevant to engaging and advancing the educational needs of students with disabilities. The emphasis is placed on evidenced-based practices that have been found to be most effective in the provision of top quality special education services.

Our motivation for writing this book comes from several concerns:

- Our understanding that, as the number of special education students grows, the educators tasked with supporting them in an inclusion setting may not have the tools to do so.
- Our knowledge that a current shortage of special education teachers may cause subpar educational opportunities for our neediest students.

- Our belief that all students, especially those who fall within the IDEA disability categories, should receive equal access to academic instruction, which occurs when best practice and research-based strategies are shared.
- Our interest in furthering the conversation surrounding special education, explicitly teaching the most important concepts, protocols, and strategies to all staff who engage with students who have exceptionalities.
- Our passion in providing equitable outcomes for all students, regardless of disability, so that they can become productive members of their immediate and global community.

To give the reader a solid foundation, this book begins with an introduction to special education that includes the description of each of the thirteen disability categories as specified in the Individuals with Disabilities Act and moves to give a clear understanding of the importance of response to intervention (RTI) as a precursor to support, and examines the individualized education plan (IEP) (IDEA, 2004; Lee, 2018). Subsequent chapters define and describe the least restrictive environment, discuss the importance of paraprofessionals for student necessity of positive home-school connections, and highlight the importance of transition planning, among other relevant special education topics.

This book was written by an experienced team whose members, at one time or another, have been parents, special education teachers, special education administrators, a superintendent, and a college professor. Through their years of service, they have worked to improve the lives of students with a variety of disabilities and exceptionalities within the classroom and the conference room. It is their collective experience that provides the basis for this book, while adding in relevant research and strategies to enhance the base of knowledge. In an age where special education has become more prevalent, and general education teachers are expected to shoulder more of the work, it behooves all educators and families to be prepared to meet these new demands. Even the most seasoned special educators will benefit from a fresh and contemporary examination of the research contained within the pages of this book.

Acknowledgments

We are indebted to Sue Clark for holding this manuscript to a rigorous standard as our highly capable and committed editor. She has been an instrumental part of our writing team through numerous books and her contributions have not gone unnoticed or unappreciated. Sue has had a long and distinguished career in public education in her own right, having long advocated for those who have confronted their own challenges, whether in the classroom or the workplace. While she would not give herself anywhere near the credit she deserves, her advocacy over the years has helped thousands of students and countless peers improve their lives immeasurably. We hope that when she finally retires, she will have the time to reflect on the many positive ways she has made a meaningful impact along the way. And while we hold her in the highest regard as a professional colleague, her gentle, kind, and supportive demeanor also makes her an invaluable friend. Thank you, Sue, for being you.

Chapter One

The Fundamentals of Special Education

Defining Disabilities and the Federal Laws that Provide Guidance

Special education is specifically designed instruction for students with disabilities. Special education includes the academic, physical, cognitive, and social-emotional instruction offered to students who have one or more disabilities (Bateman & Cline, 2016). Students require special education services or programming when they are not able to have their specific needs met in the general education classroom (Center for Parent Information & Resources, 2017a). Special education services modify or adapt content and teaching methodology to deliver instruction that meets the unique needs of the student (Center for Parent Information & Resources, 2017a).

Special education is a continuum of services that can provide instruction to students in the general education classroom as well as in the special education classroom (McManis, 2017). Students described as exceptional are those who have disabilities or extraordinary gifts and talents and may require additional supports, while twice exceptional refers to students who have both a gift and a disability (Morin, 2018a). The number of children with disabilities receiving special education and related services has steadily grown since the passage of the Education for All Handicapped Children Act in 1975 (US Department of Education, 2010b). Special education provides equal opportunities for students with disabilities in the school setting.

The first formal attempts to provide special education for children with disabilities in the United States began in the nineteenth century (Kauffman, Hallahan, & Pullen, 2017). The first schools were started for students who were blind or deaf or who had an intellectual disability and were often funded by religious groups or charities (Kauffman et al., 2017). Unless parents paid for private education, most students with disabilities, especially those with severe disabilities, were not educated. By the 1920s, most school districts in the United States had mandatory attendance laws and attempted to accommodate a wide range of student abilities (Institute of Medicine, 1997). Many students with disabilities, however, were left out of school completely.

The first federal legislation involving education was passed in 1965. Called the Elementary and Secondary Education Act (ESEA), this piece of legislation delineated how students would be taught and how federal funding would be given to states that used the monies to promote an equal and quality education for all students (Paul, 2016). ESEA has been reauthorized several times since its inception, most recently with the Every Student Succeeds Act (ESSA) (Klein, 2016). ESSA provides mandates and guidance to schools regarding appropriate public school education.

In 1975, the federal government passed the Education for All Handicapped Children Act, which later became the Individuals with Disabilities Education Act (IDEA) and mandated appropriate education for all students with disabilities in public education and students with disabilities started being included in the general education curriculum (Lee, 2018).

The Americans with Disabilities Act (ADA) was created and signed into law in 1990 to protect the rights of all persons with disabilities. While it is not specifically designed to address the needs of school children in academic and behavioral ways, it does address the needs all people with disabilities may have in other ways such as transportation, and access to buildings, bathrooms and other settings (ADA National Network, 2015). The ADA has five sections that offer guidance to include employment, state and local government, public accommodations, telecommunications, and miscellaneous provisions (ADA National Network, 2015).

While ESSA describes the mandates that pertain to public schools and the ADA focuses on public spaces, special education in the United States is governed by IDEA and Section 504 of the Rehabilitation Act (Section 504) (Rothstein & Johnson, 2013).

INDIVIDUALS WITH DISABILITIES EDUCATION ACT

The Education for All Handicapped Children Act went through major changes in 1997 and again in 2004, where the name was changed to the Individuals with Disabilities Education Improvement Act (Osborne & Russo, 2014). State laws are generally parallel to the IDEA and often use identical language. State laws can provide more for students with disabilities but not less than the federally mandated IDEA provides (Osborne & Russo, 2014).

The IDEA guarantees access to free appropriate public education (FAPE) in the least restrictive environment (LRE) to every qualifying child with a disability, which emphasizes special education and related services designed to meet the student's unique needs to prepare him or her for further education, employment, and independent living (Bateman & Bateman, 2014). The 2004 amendment of IDEA led to several improvements for students with disabilities to include an increased emphasis on access to the general education curriculum, transition planning, services for students birth to age five, and supports for the accountability of achievement (University of Kansas: School of Education, 2018a).

The IDEA upholds and protects the rights of infants, toddlers, children, and youth with disabilities and their families (Osborne & Russo, 2014). Since 1975, the United States has progressed from excluding almost 1.8 million children in public schools with disabilities, to providing special education and related services to more than 6.9 million students with disabilities, specifically designed to meet their individual needs (Turnbull, Huerta, & Stowe, 2009).

Students qualifying under the IDEA must be between the ages of three and 21 and have a qualifying diagnosed disability (Hall, Quinn, & Gollnick, 2018). The 13 disabilities defined by IDEA include autism, deaf-blindness, deafness, emotional disturbance, hearing impairment, intellectual disability, multiple disabilities, orthopedic impairment, other health impairment, specific learning disability, speech or language impairment, traumatic brain injury, and visual impairment to include blindness (Lee, 2018).

Disability Categories

Nationally, there were 5.85 million US students between the ages of six and 21 receiving special education services during the 2013–2014 school year (National Center for Education Statistics, 2018). The IDEA described 13 disability categories can be used to diagnose infants, toddlers, preschoolers, and young students who are eligible to receive special education services (Lee, 2018; US Department of Education, 2010a).

To be eligible for an Individualized Education Plan (IEP), a student must qualify under one of the 13 disabilities under IDEA. In some instances, a student may meet the criteria for more than one disability category, thereby identifying one as primary and the other as secondary (Cohen, 2009). It is important to note, however, that to qualify for special education services, the student must not only have one or more disabilities, the disability must cause an adverse effect to the student's educational performance.

Autism

Autism is a developmental disability that significantly affects verbal and nonverbal communication, and social interaction and affects 1 in 59 children (Centers for Disease Control and Prevention, 2018; National Institute of Mental Health, n.d.). Autism is generally evident before age three and adversely affects a child's educational performance. There is a wide range of symptoms for autism, and the severity can vary greatly. Students, for example, can have above average intelligence, aggressive behavior, self-injurious behavior, difficulty with pragmatic language, and a lack of social relations (National Institute of Mental Health, n.d.). Other characteristics often associated with autism are engaging in repetitive activities and stereotypical movements, resistance to change in routine, and unusual response to sensory experiences (Special Education Guide, 2018). Typically, a psychiatrist, clinical psychologist, physician or other qualified professional makes an autism diagnosis (National Autistic Society, 2018).

Blindness or Visual Impairment

Students in this category have special learning needs in areas requiring functional use of vision. As of 2016, the number of students afflicted with a visual impairment was greater than 62,500 (American Printing House for the Blind, 2016). Ultimately, a visual impairment involves an issue with sight, which interferes with a student's academic achievement. There are several conditions that can cause visual impairments and conditions can vary in severity. Conditions can include near- and farsightedness, congenital cataracts, and strabismus (Center for Parent Information & Resources, 2017b). With such a variety within the disability category, there are common signs of a visual impairment that include irregular eye movement, unusual habits such as frequently rubbing eyes or holding items abnormally close to the eye to view it (Center for Parent Information & Resources, 2017b). Academic challenges for students with visual impairments could include reading assigned tests, operating educational tools such as a computer, and safely maneuvering around the classroom independently.

Deaf-Blindness

If a child has only two disabilities and those disabilities are deafness and blindness, and the child is not reported as having a developmental delay, that child must be reported under the category "deaf-blindness." The term refers to a person who has some degree of loss in both vision and hearing, yet the amount of loss varies by individual (Center for Parent Information & Resources, 2015a). About half of individuals with deaf-blindness in the United States have a genetic condition called Usher Syndrome which causes children to eventually lose both vision and hearing; however, other causes include birth trauma, illness or injuries such as stroke, meningitis, or a head trauma (Center for Parent Information & Resources, 2015a). The simultaneous hearing and visual impairments can cause severe communication and other developmental and education needs that often need to be accommodated in programs specifically built for children with deaf-blindness.

Deaf and Hard of Hearing

Any individual with a hearing loss of great than 90 decibels is considered deaf or hard of hearing (Center for Parent Information & Resources, 2015c). It is important to note that the difference between this category and that of hearing impairment is the degree to which the impairment occurs. There are four types of hearing loss to include conductive, sensorineural, mixed, and inner ear and each may also be defined in terms of severity—mild, moderate, severe, and profound (Center for Parent Information & Resources, 2015c). Some individuals have congenital deafness or hard of hearing—in that it began before or at birth; whereas those individuals with an acquired hearing loss may have had an abundance of ear infections, fluid buildup, or head trauma (Center for Parent Information & Resources, 2015c).

Emotional Disturbance

According to the Parent Center for Information & Resources (2017c), students with an emotional disturbance may exhibit

   a. An inability to learn that cannot be explained by intellectual, sensory, or health factors.
   b. The inability to build or maintain satisfactory interpersonal relationships with peers and teachers.
   c. Inappropriate types of behavior or feelings under normal circumstances.
   d. A general pervasive mood of unhappiness or depression.
   e. A tendency to develop physical symptoms or fears associated with personal or school problems.

In simpler terms this category covers both an emotional disturbance associated with mental health or severe behavioral disorders that occur over a long period of time.

"Emotional disturbances" is an umbrella term to include eating disorders, attention-deficit/hyperactivity disorder (ADHD) and disruptive behaviors, anxiety disorders, bipolar or manic depression, conduct disorders, obsessive-compulsive disorder (OCD), and psychotic disorders (Center for Parent Information and Resources, 2017c). The student must exhibit the behavioral characteristics listed chronically in a severe form. While the criteria are primarily focused on behavior, schizophrenia is also referenced as qualifying condition. Educating students diagnosed with an emotional disturbance can be challenging. A functional behavioral assessment (FBA) can help identify what the student's behavior is communicating so that an effective behavioral intervention plan (BIP) can be developed (Collins & Zirkel, 2016).

Hearing Impairment

An impairment in hearing, whether permanent or fluctuating, that adversely affects a child's educational performance, but that is not included under the definition of deafness, is reflective of this disability (American Speech-Language-Hearing Association [ASHA], n.d.). A hearing loss above 90 decibels is considered deafness, which means that a hearing loss below 90 decibels is classified as a hearing impairment (American Speech-Language-Hearing Association [ASHA], n.d.). Hearing loss falls into the same four subcategories as the category of deaf and hard of hearing (National Dissemination Center for Children with Disabilities [NICHCY], 2010). The accommodations for each subcategory are different. Students with conductive hearing loss, which is the outer, or middle ear, for example, can utilize amplifying assistive technologies such as hearing aids to improve hearing.

Hearing loss is categorized as slight, mild, moderate, severe or profound and the category is chosen based on the student's ability to hear the frequencies associated with speech in conversations (National Dissemination Center for Children with Disabilities [NICHCY], 2010). Students with hearing impairments may experience difficulty taking notes while listening to lectures, participating in classroom discussions, watching educational videos, and doing oral presentations.

Intellectual Disability

A student with an intellectual disability has significantly subaverage general intellectual functioning, existing concurrently with deficits in adaptive behavior and manifested during the developmental period, that adversely affects a child's educational performance and deficits in adaptive behavior (American Psychiatric Association, 2017). The causes of intellectual disabilities can vary but can include issues in pregnancy, complications at birth, genetic conditions, and early health issues such as contact with lead or mercury (Wenzel, 2017). In 2012, the federal government enacted legislation changing the term mental retardation to intellectual disability in all federal law to better reflect the disability and reduce negative connotations (Federal Register, 2013).

An IQ below 70 to 75 indicates an intellectual disability. Deficits in ability can include everyday tasks such as using the restroom, getting dressed, the ability to participate in a conversation, and difficulty following social norms. Students with intellectual disabilities often have difficulty remembering, delayed developmental milestones, difficulty utilizing problem-solving skills, and understanding consequences to actions (American Psychiatric Association, 2017). An intellectual disability affects students across all aspects of life including the classroom. Students with an intellectual disability require ample time to master concepts, have difficulty understanding new concepts, and difficulty completing new complex tasks (Prater, 2016).

Multiple Disabilities

This disability category is defined by concomitant impairments (such as intellectual disability–blindness or intellectual disability–orthopedic impairment), the combination of which causes such severe educational needs that children cannot be accommodated in special education programs solely for one of the impairments (Center for Parent Information & Resources, 2015b). This category does not include deaf-blindness. At times, the cause may be due to premature birth, infections, injuries, poor development, or chromosomal abnormalities (Center for Parent Information & Resources, 2015b). Given that there are multiple disability category combinations, possible multiple disabilities encompass a broad range of traits and the severity poses more difficulties. Several common characteristics include challenges with mobility, a need for assistance with everyday activities, and limited communication skills (Center for Parent Information & Resources, 2015b).

Orthopedic Impairment

An orthopedic impairment is "a severe orthopedic impairment that adversely affects a child's educational performance" (Project IDEAL, 2013a). Orthopedic impairments involve physical disabilities, which could affect the academic process. Orthopedic impairments can be caused by birth defects, disease, or other causes. Examples could include poliomyelitis, bone tuberculosis, cerebral palsy, amputation, or burns that cause contractures. Although the exact regulation for an orthopedic impairment varies, an evaluation is required. The process includes a medical assessment performed by a qualified physician and an explanation of how the impairment would impact the child's academic performance (Project IDEAL, 2013a). The variability in conditions with orthopedic impairments can be extremely diverse. Some possible barriers within the academic setting could include communicating effectively, difficulty navigating the school, and difficulty participating in specific active classroom activities (Project IDEAL, 2013a).

Other Health Impairment

A student with a health impairment is described as "having limited strength, vitality, or alertness, including a heightened alertness to environmental stimuli, that results in limited alertness with respect to the educational environment, that is due to chronic or acute health problems" (Special Education Guide, 2018, n.p.). Examples of health impairments might include "asthma, attention deficit disorder or attention deficit hyperactivity disorder, diabetes, epilepsy, a heart condition, hemophilia, lead poisoning, leukemia, nephritis, rheumatic fever, sickle cell anemia, and Tourette syndrome" (National Dissemination Center for Children with Disabilities [NICHCY], 2012, n.p.). To qualify for special education services the student's health impairment must adversely affect his or her academic performance.

Specific Learning Disability

Specific learning disability is the eligibility category with the largest number of students (Cohen, 2009). A specific learning disability is a disorder in

> one or more of the basic psychological processes involved in understanding or in using language, spoken or written, that may manifest itself in the imperfect ability to listen, think, speak, read, write, spell, or to do mathematical calculations, including conditions such as perceptual disabilities, brain injury, minimal brain dysfunction, dyslexia, and developmental aphasia. Specific learning disability does not include learning problems that are primarily the result of visual, hearing, or motor disabilities, of intellectual disability, of emotional disturbance, or of environmental, cultural, or economic disadvantage. (Westwood, 2017, n.p.)

To qualify for a specific learning disability the student's learning deficit cannot be better explained by another disability, such as a health disability, or a cultural disadvantage.

Speech or Language Impairment

A communication disorder is included in one of the speech language subcategories, which include a fluency disorder, impaired articulation, language impairment, or a voice impairment (Project IDEAL, 2013b, n.p.). If a child fails to meet milestones set by the ASHA and testing proves a disability that affects academic progress, then the child may qualify for a speech disability (National Institute on Deafness and Other Communication Disabilities, 2017). A suspected impairment should always be evaluated by a speech language pathologist to avoid misdiagnosis since many other disabilities, such as autism, can include communication difficulties (Prelock, Hutchins, & Glascoe, 2008).

Speech and language disabilities tend to emerge at a young age and the earlier a child is diagnosed and receives services the more effective services tend to be (Prelock et al., 2008). Speech impairments and language delays can have a profound impact on a student's ability to function. Language delays can present themselves in deficits involving receptive language, expressive language, pragmatic or social language (Elzouki, Harfi, & Nazer, 2012). Speech and language skills are critical to learning and interacting with other students, staff, and the community. Students can qualify for special education under the speech and language impairment category without needing special education instruction of any kind.

Traumatic Brain Injury

Students in this category "acquired an injury to the brain caused by an external physical force, resulting in total or partial functional disability or psychosocial impairment, or both, that adversely affects a child's educational performance" (IDEA, 2007, n.p.). This does not include brain injuries induced by birth trauma, conditions that worsen over time, or those that are hereditary (IDEA, 2007). Traumatic brain injuries may cause injury or disruption to "cognition; language; memory; attention; reasoning; abstract thinking; judgment; problem solving; sensory, perceptual, and motor abilities; psychosocial behavior; physical functions; information processing; and speech" (IDEA, 2007, n.p.). Traumatic brain injuries may have a wide range of associated traits to include mental, physical, and emotional issues. Students with traumatic brain injury could have difficulty concentrating, long- and short-term memory issues, physical problems, and social differences (Stocchetti & Zanier, 2016).

These 13 categories provide guidance to the team that confirms the disability and takes the next steps toward writing the individualized education plan or the 504 plan; however, students must also require specifically designed instruction to receive FAPE in the LRE (Texas Education Agency, 2018).

INDIVIDUALIZED EDUCATION PLANS AND 504 PLANS

To receive special education services, students need to be determined eligible as specified by federal law. Every school district has the legal duty to identify and evaluate children who may need special education, including students who are homeless, highly mobile, migrant, wards of the state, and those who attend both public and private schools (Friend, 2018). Evaluations determine a child's eligibility for special education and give the team the information required to design the child's individualized education program. Students will be subsequently evaluated at least every three years following their initial evaluation. If a family is not satisfied with the testing or feels the student's needs have changed since the previous test, they can request additional evaluations, including an independent evaluation from an outside provider (Hoover & Patton, 2017).

Both an IEP and a 504 plan are intended to protect a student with a disability to ensure that he or she is learning in the LRE and is given the tools to be successful (Friend, 2018). Both are detailed plans that are developed in collaboration with families and the school to outline how a student with a disability will learn; however, there are significant differences between an IEP and a 504 plan that include the eligibility, the laws they are covered under, and the services they provide to students (Hoover & Patton, 2017).

Individualized Education Plan

An IEP is a document required by law that outlines a student's instructional goals, objectives, accommodations, general class participation, and necessary related services to meet the needs connected to the disability identified as the basis for special education eligibility and placement (Hoover & Patton, 2017). The IDEA requires schools to provide special education and related services to eligible students (Hoover & Patton, 2017). To be eligible, the student's school performance must be adversely affected by one of 13 labeled disabilities (IDEA, 2004). The IEP provides families and educators with a guide for the teaching and learning of a student with a disability who has been properly placed for services consistent with state and federal laws (DeBettencourt & Howard, 2017).

The design, presentation, and formatting of IEPs vary; however, several content items are mandated by the IDEA, including a student's present level of academic achievement and functional performance, measurable annual goals, description of services (special education, related services, supplemental aids and services), general education curriculum participation, progress monitoring, participation considerations in state and district assessments, and transition services (DeBettencourt & Howard, 2017).

Once a student is found eligible for special education services, an IEP must be developed (Friend, 2018). The IEP process is a cooperative approach that brings together families, students, general education teachers, special education teachers, and related service providers. Each member of the team has an important and unique perspective of the student's strengths, weaknesses, and needs, and should be treated as equal partners as the information available will help make important decisions for students with disabilities.

The IEP should represent the parents' concerns and vision, which will assist the student to work toward independence and overall success (Tomlinson, 2014). As the team works collaboratively toward the creation of an IEP that fits the student's individual needs, the school will integrate the opinions of different professionals to provide the family with a proposal that includes the services required for student success (Tomlinson, 2014).

Section 504 of the Rehabilitation Act of 1973

Similar to an IEP, a 504 service plan is an accommodation plan developed for students who have an identified disability and have challenges that are impacting their learning (US Department of Education, 2018). The impact requires modifications, accommodations, and adjustments within the general education setting, but does not require specifically designed instruction and special education services like an IEP does. To be eligible for a 504 plan, students must have a disability, which include various learning or attention issues, and a disability that interferes with the student's ability to learn in the general education classroom (US Department of Education, 2010a). A student who does not qualify for an IEP may qualify for a 504 plan (Braaten, 2018).

Students and their families are responsible for ensuring that school officials are aware of the student's impairment and need for specific accommodations for specific activities (Bateman & Bateman, 2014). Prior to receiving accommodations, students or their families must prove that there is a need for accommodations, such as learning disabilities. Creating a written Section 504 Service Plan explaining the student's accommodations is not mandated, although many districts and school administrators choose to engage with families and write one together (Bateman & Cline, 2016).

A 504 service plan should include a list of who is assisting in creating the plan, demographic information of the student, a detailed description of the student's impairment and an explanation of how it impedes the student's progress, and a list of the accommodations and services being offered to the student, which includes the frequency and who will provide the services (Friend, 2018). Students who qualify under Section 504 are entitled to reasonable accommodations that will allow them to better access the curriculum. Administration is not required to make accommodations that go beyond what is considered reasonable, such as exposing staff to risk, requiring substantial modifications to the school's mission, or providing an accommodation that is excessively expensive (Russo & Osborne, 2008).

ADDITIONAL CONSIDERATIONS UNDER IDEA

Students may also need related services to benefit from the special education placement (Osborne & Russo, 2014). Not all students who receive special education require related services. Related services are provided in addition to special education to help students receive educational benefits from the special education program. Classroom structures, support personnel, and school administration also play important roles when considering a plan for a student who presents with special education needs.

Procedural Safeguards

The IDEA includes an intricate system of procedural safeguards to protect the rights of children with disabilities and their parents. The purpose of the safeguards is to ensure that families have opportunities to be involved in the education of their children. Schools are required to provide parents or guardians written notice, and must receive consent prior to the child being evaluated, initial placement, or initiating changes in placement (Bateman & Cline, 2016). Additionally, families must be given the opportunity to participate in the development of their child's IEP and the decision of placement.

Families can request an Independent Educational Evaluation (IEE), which is an evaluation conducted by a qualified examiner who is not employed by the school district responsible for the education of the student (Bateman & Cline, 2016). This can be requested at the district's expense if the parents disagree with the district's evaluation. Families can have independent evaluations conducted at their own expense at any time and are entitled to one IEE at public expense each time the district conducts an evaluation on the student (Bateman & Cline, 2016).

Parents or guardians have the right to review their child's record within 10 days of requesting it and prior to any IEP meeting or due process hearing (Cohen, 2009). If parents are unfamiliar with the documents, a professionally qualified school representative will be provided to explain the records. The parents or guardians, eligible student, authorized school personnel, and state or federal official are allowed to see the student's record without specific, informed, written consent. The family's representative, such as an advocate, can review a student's record when providing written informed consent (Cohen, 2009).

Least Restrictive Environment and Zero Reject

The IDEA requires that, to the maximum extent possible, children with disabilities are educated with children who are not disabled (Friend, 2018). Students should only be removed from the regular education environment when the severity of the disability prevents the student from achieving satisfactory results, even with supplementary aids and services (Friend, 2018). The IDEA has a strong preference for educating students with disabilities in regular classes with appropriate aids and supports. The IEP must state the specific special education and related services to be provided for the student to be able to participate in the general education classroom, which is ultimately the LRE (Friend, 2018).

Historically, students with disabilities have been denied access to opportunities due to the severity of their disability (University of Kansas: School of Education, 2018a). In response, the IDEA mandated that local educational agencies must provide education for every student with a disability regardless of the condition or diagnosis and that schools receiving federal funding must educate all students with disabilities (Friend, 2018). This applies to all students, regardless of the severity of the disability, since no child can be excluded from public school.

Continuum of Services and Least Restrictive Environment

The issue of appropriate placement of children with disabilities has always generated considerable controversy and debate (Gargiulo & Metcalf, 2013). Federal legislation mandates that services be provided to students in the LRE, and that students with disabilities should be educated in the setting that most closely approximates the general education classroom, and yet still meets the student's unique needs (Friend, 2018). Federal courts mandated that students with disabilities are included in both the academic and the extracurricular programs of the general education to the maximum extent appropriate (Gargiulo & Metcalf, 2013). The student's placement must be determined individually and is based on the student's educational needs, not their disability.

Effective delivery of special education services requires an array or continuum of placement options that are customized to the individual requirements of each student (Gargiulo, 2016). Inclusion is not a requirement as it is not always appropriate for students, but it should be the first option considered on where special education services will be provided. Students should only be removed from the general education class when it is necessary for the student to receive an appropriate education.

The education continuum for special education services goes from the LRE, which would be the general education setting, to receiving support in class, to pull-out services, to pull-out special education classes with mainstream opportunities, to day schools, to residential clusters, to hospital schools, and lastly to homebound services (Gargiulo, 2016). As the needs of the student changes, so should the educational placement, which is why there is a continuum of service possibilities available to students.

Related Services

The term "related services" refers to

> transportation, and such developmental, corrective, and other supportive services, which could include speech language pathology, audiology services, interpreting services, psychological services, physical and occupational

therapy, . . . therapeutic recreation, social work services, school nurse services designed to enable a child with a disability to receive a free appropriate public education as described in the individualized education program of the child, counseling services, orientation and mobility services, and medical services. (IDEA, n.d., n.p.)

Related services may help a child meet educational goals, yet it does not always provide specialized instruction. Students can receive related services through an IEP or a 504 plan (Massachusetts Department of Elementary and Secondary Education, 2018). The special education team decides if related services are necessary and in some cases students who qualify for special education services do not qualify for related services and vice versa (Wrightslaw, 2018). Related services help students benefit from general education and often make it easier for students to participate in class and in activities that are outside of school.

In addition to the federal mandates surrounding the IDEA, there are best practices and research-based strategies that all special education teams use to ensure student success. These include classroom structure, support personnel, and school administration.

Classroom Structure

For most students with diagnosed disabilities, they spend most of the day in the general education classroom (Johnson-Harris & Mundschenk, 2014). This has not always been the case, and this change has been occurring over the past 50 years (Bateman & Cline, 2016). Federal laws have mandated that students with disabilities are entitled to be included in the general education classrooms, which is the LRE to the maximum extent possible (Lee, 2018). The educational services provided to students must be appropriate and allow the student to make progress in the curriculum that is created to meet the student's specific learning needs (Lee, 2018).

Inclusive education provides students with disabilities access to the standard curriculum in the general education classroom (Bryant, Smith, & Bryant, 2016). The inclusive setting is the LRE and allows students with disabilities to be educated alongside their nondisabled peers. Inclusion should always be considered when making decisions regarding student placement. When in the general education setting, however, students with disabilities require appropriate accommodations and modifications to meet their specific learning needs (Tomlinson, 2014).

Inclusive education has many interpretations and strategies that allow it to be successful for students. In full inclusion, students receive all educational services in the general education classroom regardless of the changes to curriculum or related services they receive (Boyle & Topping, 2012). A student in full inclusion, for example, would receive speech and/or language services from a speech language pathologist (SLP) in the general education classroom rather than removing the student into an individual setting.

Inclusion is also carried out through the method of co-teaching in which a general education teacher and special education teacher work collaboratively to provide interventions across the academic content for all the students in the class (Boyle & Topping, 2012). One approach to allow students with varying abilities to access the curriculum is through the universal design for learning (UDL) approach, which "guides the design of instructional goals, assessments, methods, and materials that can be customized and adjusted to meet individual needs" (CAST, 2018, n.p.).

Although the general education classroom and inclusion is the LRE that does not mean it is what is most appropriate for all students. Students with more severe disabilities are often unable to access the curriculum or make progress in the general education setting and require more specialized small group instruction in the special education setting.

The pull-out model offers a more restrictive environment than inclusive services. Pull-out services include resource rooms and partially self-contained classes (Massachusetts Department of Elementary and Secondary Education, 2018). In this model students leave the general education classroom for less than 50% of the school day to receive individualized instruction from a special education teacher or related service provider (Swanson, Harris, & Graham, 2013).

For many students who receive most of the education in general education classes, the resource room is the option for pull-out special education services. Resource room instruction often consists of small group instruction, which focuses on a specific area of intense intervention such as reading, written language, or math problem solving (Bryant et al., 2016). The extent of pull-out services should be based on the individual student's need and follow the student's IEP. When pull-out services are necessary, the student's schedule should be created in conjunction with the special education teacher, related service providers, and general education teachers, so that the services are implemented with consideration to the least disruptive option for general education participation (Burns, 2007).

A substantially separate classroom, also referred to as a self-contained classroom, is for students with significant disabilities for whom the general education classroom or resource room is not an option (Braaten, 2018). Substantially separate environments serve students who require significant modifications to the curriculum, small class size, and low student to teacher ratios. The goal of an effective self-contained placement is to gradually increase the amount of time the student spends in the general education environment, if possible (Frey, 2018). Students placed in a self-contained classroom should spend time in the general education environment with peers even if it is for the social aspect through specials such as art, gym, lunch, or recess with the support of a special education teacher or paraprofessional (Frey, 2018).

Support Personnel

There is growing recognition of the importance of professionals working together in the best interest of the student regardless of the different disciplines they represent (Gargiulo & Bouck, 2018). Many students receiving special education services have complex needs that require the interventions, resources, and clinical skills offered by different professions. Successful implementation of special education services requires the special education team to work collaboratively in the best interest of the student. Professional cooperation and partnership are the key to delivering efficient and integrated services (Gargiulo & Bouck, 2018). Meaningful collaboration includes voluntary participation in the relationship, along with shared goals, accountability, and resources (Friend & Cook, 2013).

The general education setting is becoming more inclusive as districts develop strategies for assisting general education teachers to serve students with disabilities. The general education teachers can provide services to students with disabilities and accommodate the curriculum to meet the needs of the various learners in the classroom (Tomlinson, 2014). The general education teacher will benefit from the support of the special education teacher. This may take the form of consultation that is focused on the problem-solving process and the modification of teaching strategies or learning environment to accommodate the needs of students with disabilities (Tomlinson, 2014).

School Administration

School administrators, or principals play a pivotal role for the improvement of educational opportunities for all students, especially those with disabilities (DiPaola & Walther-Thomas, 2003). The administrator's values, beliefs, and personal characteristics inspire school staff to work toward fulfilling the school's mission of an inclusive environment. Administrators collaborate with other school staff to develop effective learning communities and ensure that staff and students have the support and resources needed to be successful. Successful administrators encourage innovation, collaboration, and professional growth, which can lead to successful academic outcomes for all students, including students with disabilities (Stephens, 2015).

Administrative leadership has been found to be the most powerful predictor of positive teacher attitudes about inclusive education practices of students with disabilities (Mngo & Mngo, 2018). Principals who focus on instructional issues, demonstrate administrative support for special education, and provide high-quality training for teachers to produce enhanced outcomes for students with disabilities. Although administrators may not have explicit academic interactions with students with disabilities, the attitude they model toward inclusive education and students with disabilities can make immense positive change within the school setting.

FINAL THOUGHTS

Over time, several federal mandates have paved the way for students with disabilities to access public education in ways that were not possible prior to 1975. The Americans with Disabilities Act, the Individuals with Disabilities Act, Section 504 and the current version ESSA, known as the Every Student Succeeds Act all play a part in creating a solid foundation for academic success. Each targets a specific set of concepts and student needs, while giving specific directions on how to move forward for students with disabilities. While the ADA controls public spaces, the IDEA lays out specifically how to move through the process of identifying students and giving them their just-right education. Together, these pieces of legislature continue to guide states, school districts, administrators, and trained professionals as they help students succeed.

Understanding the 13 disability categories helps to provide a solid base of knowledge that, along with the specific mandates within IDEA, provides special education team members with the information needed to make appropriate decisions for students who come up for review under the special education process. The IEP and 504 process are complex, and teams are smart to consider all options prior to creating a plan.

POINTS TO REMEMBER

- General education in the United States is governed by the ESSA, while special education is governed by the IDEA. The ADA provides guidance on public venues and other systems.
- There are 13 specified disabilities under the IDEA umbrella. To qualify for special education students must have one or more disabilities that prevents the student from making adequate progress in the classroom and adversely affects the student's educational performance.
- Special education is specifically designed academic, physical, cognitive, and social-emotional instruction for students with disabilities.
- When considering an IEP or 504, teams must consider the least restrictive setting and the continuum of services as ways to provide the student with everything necessary for learning.

- The special education team consists of teachers, administration, families, service providers, psychologists, social workers, and anyone else who has concerns or cares for the child in question.

Chapter Two

Response to Intervention and Multi-Tiered Systems of Support

A Close Examination of the Prereferral Process

In 2015 there were approximately 6.7 million children ages three to 21 receiving special education services in the United States, which is 13% of the student population (National Center for Education Statistics, 2018). Effective response to intervention (RTI) program implementation focuses on individual attention to the needs of each student and will limit the number of unwarranted students being recommended for special education testing (Stahl, 2016). Special education is extremely expensive and significantly reducing the number of special education students directs resources toward general education and services more students (Hehir, Grindal, & Eidelman, 2012).

When students struggle in school, research suggests that RTI should be the first step in the process to help the student (Stahl, 2016). Also known as a multi-tiered system of support (MTSS), RTI ensures additional time and support needed to learn at high levels through timely targeted systematic interventions to all students who demonstrate the need (Buffum, Mattos, & Weber, 2012). MTSS and RTI bring together high-quality teaching and assessment methods, so students who are not successful when presented with one set of instruction methods can be given the chance to succeed by using other practices.

The earlier schools can intervene the greater chance there is to effectively reduce and eliminate the achievement gap. When helping students at risk, structured support programs that provide flexibility for the learner are most effective (Lemons, Fuchs, Gilbert, & Fuchs, 2014). RTI supports both academic and behavior (social) skills equally as it integrates a school-wide, multi-level prevention system to maximize student achievement and reduce behavior problems. RTI is not one intervention or method but rather a set of scientifically based procedures that can be used to make educational decisions (RTI Action Network, n.d.). The four essential components of RTI are screening, progress monitoring, a multilevel prevention system, and data-based decision making (National Center on Response to Intervention, 2010).

The components that make up RTI include data collection and high-quality teaching strategies and although they have been used for many years, they had not previously been organized into the system labeled RTI. The term first showed up in federal law in 2004 when the IDEA was last reauthorized (Lee, 2018). The RTI process was put forward as an alternative method of identifying students with learning disabilities. The goal of RTI was to decrease the number of students being placed in special education by providing struggling students with early interventions to meet their specific needs and to accelerate progress (Vaughn, Denton, & Fletcher, 2010). Through screening, diagnostics, and classroom-based instruction, legislation mandated schools to identify and teach at-risk students in ways that they can learn best throughout their school career (Klein, 2015). A student at risk refers to those who have met the criteria for potentially being at risk of facing learning difficulties (Cortiella & Horowitz, 2014).

THE SCREENING PROCESS

Most school districts use RTI to intervene prior to a special education referral (Kauffman et al., 2017). Screening identifies students who are not making progress or are at risk for poor learning outcomes and require additional assessment and instruction. By providing prereferral interventions fewer students will need special education services (Hauerwas, Brown, & Scott, 2013). Screening takes into consideration student strengths and struggles, cultural responsiveness, and linguistics (Carr & Bertrando, 2012).

Universal screening is the first component of RTI and it is used at the beginning of the year or when a new student arrives during the school year as well as at various times during the year, to identify students who are struggling with grade-level concepts or skills (Hughes & Dexter, n.d.; Hughes & Dexter, 2011). Universal screening determines a student's baseline, so progress can be assessed. Universal screening measures consist of brief assessments focused on skills that are highly predictive of future outcomes such as phonological awareness (Jenkins, 2007).

The use of at least two screening measures is highly recommended as the use of a single measure can result in a false positive. Using two or more screening methods can enhance the accuracy of the screening processes and ensures that schools are not exhausting their resources by providing instruction to an inflated percent of the student population (Jenkins, 2007). Common forms of universal screenings are curriculum-based measures, such as Dynamic Indicators of Basic Early Literacy Skills (DIBELS), and schoolwide behavior norms (University of Oregon, Center on Teaching and Learning, 2018).

Teachers analyze scores to look for students who fall below the cut point. A cut point or cut score is a selected point on the scorer scale of a test and is often classified into categories such as basic, proficient, or advanced (Dynamic Measurement Group, 2016; Zieky & Perie, 2006). Students that fall below the cut point alert a teacher of potentially at-risk students. Cut points are usually selected by districts to determine if students need additional testing or intervention (Zieky & Perie, 2006).

When students score slightly below the cut point on a screening measure schools may give additional screening measures or monitor student progress for six to eight weeks to see if they need intervention (National Center for Response to Intervention, 2010). Additional screenings can save time and efforts by preventing unnecessary interventions and screening errors. Universal screenings have two common errors to include false positive, which is when a student is deemed at risk when they are not and false negative, which is when a student is deemed not at risk yet performs poorly (Hughes & Dexter, 2011).

Effective universal screening measures include sensitivity, defined as the degree to which a screening mechanism reliably identifies at-risk students (Hughes & Dexter, n.d.). To ensure educators can use the assessment, it should be brief, simple, and quickly identify students to maximize instructional time (Hughes & Dexter, 2011). The screening should be performed in a large classroom group by the general education teacher (Hughes & Dexter, n.d.). Consequential validity is defined as not harming the student while simultaneously linking the intervention to safe practices (Hughes & Dexter, 2011). It is important to use universal screening measures consistently. Consistency is key; thus, it is important to keep assessment measures the same during the school year.

PROBLEM-SOLVING TEAMS

Problem-solving teams can be labeled as student support teams, student success teams, child study teams, or teacher assessment teams, and these teams help teachers get additional assistance for students who are not succeeding with the current level of support (Morin, 2018b). The team should be composed of administrators, teachers, and specialists with an array of expertise. The main purpose of the team is to facilitate data-driven decision making (Morin, 2018b).

RTI teams should have a problem-solving protocol in place to assure an efficient and effective RTI program that works to benefit the students served through the program (King & Coughlin, 2016). Problem solving is one way to help RTI members assess problems within the RTI program, determine factors contributing to the problem, identify steps to solve the problem, and evaluate the RTI process (King & Coughlin, 2016). Decisions made based on a problem- solving plan are data based on each child's individualized current instructional level (Turse & Albrecht, 2015). The team reviews student performance data to identify and determine learning problems, develop interventions, and evaluate the effects of the interventions.

The Problem Solving Model (PSM) is comprised of four steps that are used in order and can be repeated over time (MDCPS Office of Academics, Accountability & School Improvement, 2014).

- *Problem Identification:* The problem should be stated in objective, measurable terms using direct measures of academics or behavior. The focus should be on teachable skills that can be measured and changed through the process.
- *Problem Analysis:* The team investigates why the problem occurs. Relevant information about the problem is gathered as to why students are not meeting expected goals. Thoughts should be geared toward instruction, curriculum, environment and the individual learner.
- *Intervention Development and Implementation:* A plan of research-based instruction or intervention plan should be created that meets individual student's needs. A good intervention plan includes specifically defined skills to be taught, measurable objectives, defined staff members who will complete various tasks, an assessment plan, and available resources.
- *Intervention Evaluation and Modification:* Reflection and evaluation of the effectiveness of each intervention. There are three outcomes for each intervention; a positive response which closes the gap, a questionable response which shows no change in the gap, and a poor response which is when the gap continues to widen with no change in rate. (MDCPS Office of Academics, Accountability & School Improvement, 2014)

Essentially, in the PSM, the intervention is defined, used for a set time frame, then reevaluated for success. If the intervention doesn't work, teachers should modify the intervention until it is successful.

MULTI-LEVEL PREVENTION SYSTEM

The purpose of organizing resources and supports into a tiered system is to assist RTI teams in identifying interventions, instructional strategies, and materials that may be effective in meeting the needs of struggling students (RTI Action Network, n.d.). The majority of RTI models used utilize a three-tier system; although it is important to note that several different RTI models have four tiers (Brown & Steege, 2011). Each tier is a supplement to the one before it. For example, someone receiving Tier 3 supports would receive those supports as a supplement to tier 1 and 2 supports, not a replacement. In four-tier models the fourth tier is special education. The common theme among all models is that there are multiple tiers of support to engage all children (Whitten, Esteves, & Woodrow, 2009).

- *Tier 1:* Demonstrates education received by all students and provides accommodations and strategies that teachers can use in the general education setting (Al Otaiba et al., 2014). These research-based class interventions are available to all students and are implemented within the general education framework. Teachers should continuously assess students to determine instructional strengths and needs.

  Of the Tier 1 students, 80–90% of them can be successful without needing further intervention (RTI Action Network, n.d.). Strategy examples include pairing visual directions with oral directions, utilize graphic organizers, provide opportunities for students to respond in a variety of ways, review and preview previously taught materials, provide additional time for classwork, homework and assessments, reduction of distraction, and positive reinforcement.
- *Tier 2:* When students do not demonstrate adequate progress through Tier 1, implementation of secondary interventions are needed. Approximately 10–15% of students benefit from more intensive interventions (Reschly, 2014). While still delivered in the general education setting, interventions vary depending on student need. This level of supplemental support is for students that require more significant, explicit, targeted, and individualized intervention plans, which will be developed to meet the needs of the specific struggling student (Job, 2016).

  The specific interventions the student receives are based on the information collected, progress monitoring, and the RTI team discussions (RTI Action Network, n.d.). The second tier of interventions occur in conjunction with the continuation of Tier 1 interventions. Strategy examples include peer tutoring, social skills group, check in and check out, technology as supplement, reading specialist intervention, small group instruction, and a point system for motivation.
- *Tier 3:* When students demonstrate significant learning discrepancies after intervention from the first two tiers more intense instruction must take place in the third tier. Often students may need intervention from Tier 3 to help remediate their skill deficits (Fuchs & Vaughn, 2012). One to five percent of students require this amount of intensive academic and behav-

ioral interventions and will require long-term intervention (Reschly, 2014). Educators responsible for this intervention require specialized training such as a psychologist, special education teacher, counselor, or Title 1 reading or math teacher.

In the third level, implementation of special education and related services provide a systematic and specialized approach outside of the general education instruction (Harlacher, Sanford, & Walker, n.d.). During a Tier 3 session, students should be mirroring the skills being taught in the general education class as well as filling skill gaps causing difficulty. Students should be given continuous corrective feedback, encouragement, and self-monitoring activities (Harlacher et al., n.d.).

Determination of intensive programs is based on the data collected within the first and second tier of RTI. Strategy examples for Tier 3 include structured breaks, intense tutoring, daily behavior forms, a functional behavior assessment, alternatives to suspension, individualized multisensory reading instruction, such as Orton-Gillingham or Reading Recovery, and implementation of a Positive Behavioral Intervention and Supports (PBIS) (Positive Behavioral Interventions & Supports, 2018a).

POSITIVE BEHAVIORAL INTERVENTIONS AND SUPPORTS

Challenging behavior in one student may reduce access to instruction in the classroom for that specific student as well as others. PBIS is a universal prevention framework for organizing evidence-based practices within the school and classroom that decrease the number of disruptive behaviors (Simonsen & Myers, 2015). This approach draws upon behavioral, social, and learning principles that have been traditionally used with individual students and is applied to the entire student body consistently across all school settings (Ditrano, 2015).

PBIS is considered an RTI approach for social and emotional behavior that can be implemented throughout all grade levels. RTI and PBIS share many common features and underlying theories to include proactively preventing problems as a more effective solution than treating problems as they arise (McIntosh & Goodman, 2016). Similar to RTI, PBIS offers a range of interventions that include universal, targeted, and intensive levels of supports that are systematically applied to students based on their level of need (Positive Behavioral Interventions & Supports, 2018a).

The PBIS framework for implementing evidence-based practices, provides a three-tiered continuum of support to students very similar to RTI (Positive Behavioral Interventions & Supports, 2018a). PBIS provides a unifying framework for designing and implementing proactive interventions that is worked into all school improvement efforts and uses data collection to inform decisions (McIntosh & Goodman, 2016). The approach is flexible to meet the unique needs of individual districts, schools, classrooms, and students. The goal is for at least 80% of the students to respond to universal supports by displaying acceptable behavior, with at most 15% of the students requiring targeted supports and 5% of students requiring intensive supports (Ditrano, 2015).

Those schools and districts that used PBIS with fidelity, documented reduced disruptive behavior, reduced bullying, increased academic achievement, increased school safety, improved teacher climate, increased social competence, and increased emotional regulation (Bradshaw, Koth, Thorton, & Leaf, 2009; Bradshaw, Waasdarp, & Leaf, 2012).

PROGRESS MONITORING

Progress monitoring is used to assess students' academic performance, to quantify a student rate of improvement or responsiveness to instruction (Reschly, 2014). Progress monitoring can be implemented with individual students or the entire class. Through progress monitoring, children can be identified as at-risk students who need assistance and can benefit from the implementation of an RTI program (Catts, Nielsen, Bridges, Lui, & Bontempo, 2015). When staff has detailed information on student strengths and weaknesses, appropriate interventions can be individualized to best fit the way a student learns. In progress monitoring, attention should focus on fidelity of implementation and selection of evidence-based tools, with considerations for cultural and linguistic responsiveness and recognition of student strengths and should occur at least monthly (Catts et al., 2015).

Districts can create implementation timelines to guide universal measurement procedures for data collection to determine each student's progress. By monitoring progress frequently, students demonstrate more improved performance (McIntosh & Goodman, 2016). Progress monitoring combines assessment and evaluation to determine student progress (Christ, Zopluoglu, Monaghen, & Van Norman, 2013). Teachers can provide additional information through behavior logs, grades, homework, and work samples. By analyzing multiple sources of data, the RTI teachers can create a comprehensive analysis of the student.

DATA-BASED DECISION MAKING

The best educational decisions are based on data. Effective RTI systems function on decisions driven by data to determine a student's instructional needs and the intensity of services needed (Reschly, 2014). Staff should use data to determine student strengths and learning gaps that will focus improvement efforts (Reschly, 2014). By using data to drive instruction, team members can have deeper conversations about the students and the data can drive decisions (Moyle, 2016).

Assessments are valuable tools for measuring current academic achievement and can play a pivotal role in the selection of effective interventions (Fan & Hansmann, 2015). To fully understand students and their needs it is important for teachers to use multiple measures in student assessment to better support decisions when determining individual interventions for students (Burns & Gibbons, 2017). Teachers and the RTI team can use additional information such as student grades, behavior logs, observations, classwork, and homework to assess the current level of performance. This global look at the student ensures that the team makes the best intervention decisions at any given time.

Data teams should have at least three members, should review progress monitoring data every four to six weeks, and follow established systematic data review procedures (Bambrick-Santoyo, 2010). The four key components of effective data collection and analysis include defining the target skill or behavior, specifying the setting where data will be collected, using an accurate data recording format, and conducting careful data analysis and interpretation (Brown & Steege, 2011).

SPECIAL EDUCATION REFERRAL

In addition to finding ways to help students succeed, RTI may be used as part of the determination process for identifying students with a variety of disabilities. Successful RTI implementation should more identify those students who truly have a specific learning disability (SLD). The number of students with an SLD fell by a margin of 2:1 in states that mandated RTI versus those that did not mandate its use (Sindelar, McCray, & Brownell, 2014).

Students who continue to show minimal or no academic growth as compared to peers after Tier 3 interventions may be considered for special education services (McIntosh & Goodman, 2016). After an RTI program has been implemented, if a student is referred for special education services, the referral is justly warranted as the student has received structured intervention through an effective program. A student who is referred for special education testing after being in the RTI tiered system has considerable data collected that provides the needed precise justification for moving to a more involved process (Young & Johnson, 2019). When an RTI program is implemented based on individual needs, students can achieve academic and behavioral success in schools.

FINAL THOUGHTS

Using an intervention program supports best practice in determining academic need. Although used independently, the introduction of the reauthorization of IDEA brought about a more formalized practice called response to intervention that sought to use data collection and research-based interventions to reduce the number of special education referrals. This was accomplished through a tiered system that gave the neediest students core instruction plus more to mitigate academic and behavioral deficits. Those students who continued to lag were then referred for special education services. PBIS is another tiered system used to proactively influence behavior in students. Together, these systems provide a foundation of support for students and teachers based on best practice and research.

POINTS TO REMEMBER

- MTSS, RTI, and PBIS all provide targeted systematic interventions.
- MTSS, RTI, and PBIS all bring together high-quality teaching through a tiered method that utilizes data and assessment to base decisions.
- Screening identifies students who are not making progress and who require additional assessment and instruction. These tiered systems limit the number of special education referrals.
- The best educational decisions are based on data collected by a variety of means and include formal assessments, informal observations, homework, and classwork.

Chapter Three

Determining the Need for Special Education Services

A Spotlight on the Assessment and Diagnostic Process

The Child Find Mandate of the IDEA requires states to find, locate, and evaluate all children who may have a disability and require special education services, including children who are highly mobile, homeless, migrant or children who are wards of the state from birth through age 21 (Dragoo, 2017). Myriad of professionals collaborate as part of a team, often referred to as a multidisciplinary team, whose responsibility it is to determine what, if any, disability is present in a student.

The team's role is crucial as it helps determine the path of a student's special education experience (Pierangelo & Giuliani, 2007). A variety of assessment tools and strategies are used to gather relevant functional, academic, and developmental information about the child. This information, including information provided by the parents, is used to determine whether the child has a disability, the child's present levels of academic achievement and functional performance and, if eligible for special education and related services, the content of the child's IEP.

REASON FOR REFERRAL

When classroom and small group interventions continue to be unsuccessful, and the student continues to have trouble, a referral for a special education evaluation may be made to determine if specifically designed instruction is more appropriate (Bateman & Cline, 2016). Referrals for determination of eligibility for special education services may be initiated by the child's parents or legal guardians, school personnel, or any other person involved in the education or care of the child.

If parents are concerned about their child's academic, social, or behavioral development and suspects that the child requires special education services, a letter should be written to the student's teacher, school principal, or the director of special education of the school district to request an evaluation (Bateman & Cline, 2016). Parents should include specific concerns, questions, and a statement of informed consent for the evaluation in the written request (Bateman & Cline, 2016).

The school may request parental permission to test a student based on teacher observations, or lack of progress. An educator could recommend students for testing for academic, social, or behavioral concerns. Prior to a recommendation for special education evaluation, most districts utilize a multi-tiered system of instruction to provide remedial support to students (McIntosh & Goodman, 2016).

Although the school may want to assess a student, signed consent from the parent is the first step (Pierangelo & Giuliani, 2006). The request describes what will be assessed and requires a parent signature. In the letter to families, the district should include an explanation of why the district is proposing testing, a description of each evaluation procedure being used, the procedural safeguards as determined by law, and sources that parents can contact to obtain assistance in understanding the provisions of IDEA (Learning Disabilities Association of America, 2018).

ASSESSMENT: DATA COLLECTION

Assessment is a broader method of data collection than testing. Testing consists of administering a set of questions to an individual to obtain a score; however, other procedures such as interviews, behavioral observations, informal assessments, and record reviews should also be used to provide a well-rounded picture of the student (Pierangelo & Giuliani, 2016).

Testing

A test is a predetermined set of questions or tasks where a variety of academic or behavioral responses are sought (Salvia, Ysseldyke, & Witmer, 2013). Standardized tests are all provided the same way regardless of who the evaluator is, so student test scores can be compared. Tests provide quantitative and qualitative information. Quantitative data refers to the scores achieved on the test, while qualitative data refers to observations made while a student is tested, such as how long they spent on individual problems, comments made, or visual behavior during testing (Salvia et al., 2013). The quantitative data provides the scores that the student achieved, while the qualitative data helps the evaluator know how the student earned their scores (Salvia et al., 2013).

Testing requirements

When conducting an individualized evaluation, the school districts must follow ethical practices. Standardized tests must assess all areas related to the suspected disability and provide relevant information that will assist the team in determining the education needs of the student (Learning Disabilities Association of America, 2018). Districts must also ensure that all standardized tests utilized have been validated for the specific purpose used and are administered by trained personnel in accordance with the protocol provided by the test publisher (Learning Disabilities Association of America, 2018). A variety of assessment tools and strategies should be used to gather functional and developmental information about the student (Learning Disabilities Association of America, 2018).

Testing Examiners and Testing Conditions

The school is mandated to test all areas of the suspected disability of a student including health, vision and hearing, social and emotional status, general intelligence, academic performance, communication abilities, and motor abilities (Taylor & Sternberg, 2012). Depending on the student's suspected disability, the student may be evaluated by any number of trained professionals to include, but not limited to, a school psychologist, SLP, occupational therapist, physical therapist, special education teacher, and reading specialist.

Testing administrators should meet the minimum requirements provided by the testing protocol. The National Association of School Psychologists (2010), for example, establishes ethical and training standards for school psychologists. At a minimum, a school psychologist must have a master's degree in school psychology and be certified or licensed by the state that he or she works in (Jacob, Decker, & Lugg, 2016). Some student achievement tests, however, only recommend that the examiner have graduate-level training in educational assessment; therefore, a teacher who graduated with a master's degree would be able to administer some tests (Jacob et al., 2016).

To obtain accurate scores from a norm-referenced test, procedures and conditions must be followed under a set of standard conditions (Salvia et al., 2013). The further an evaluation deviates from standardized procedures and conditions, the more error is introduced into the results. Testing administrators should review and be familiar with all protocols provided for each exam prior to evaluating a student; otherwise, the results will not be considered valid (Salvia et al., 2013). Specific tests, for example, do not allow evaluators to repeat questions, provide scrap paper, or rephrase directions. If an assessment is not conducted under standard conditions, a description to the extent to which it varied from standard conditions must be included in the evaluation report (Salvia et al., 2013).

Language

All tests and assessment materials used to evaluate a student must be given in a manner that is not discriminatory on a racial or cultural basis; thus, the school district must ensure that all assessment materials are provided and administered in the student's native language (OECD, 2012). An English language learner (ELL) is a student whose native or dominant language is a language other than English. If a student is referred for special education evaluation, delaying the evaluation for a specified period based on the student's language status is not permissible, and the student should be tested in their native language within the expected timeline. Additionally, all communication with families such as meeting invitations, parent rights, permission forms, and IEPs must be provided in the parents' native language (OECD, 2012).

Interpreters should be utilized throughout the special education process as they ensure that directions, questions, and answers are understood (Fenner, 2013). Most interpreters are not trained in special education assessment and should be told to use direct translation rather than paraphrasing information. If an interpreter is required to administer an assessment, the interpreter should meet with the testing evaluator prior to the testing session to review testing procedures, schedule, restrictions, and expectations (Fenner, 2013). The interpreter should translate the exact wording of the assessment, should not provide any prompting to the student, and should ask the evaluator questions as they arise. After the evaluation, the interpreter and testing evaluator should discuss the testing session. Testing in a student's first language is an important part of the assessment process (Fenner, 2013).

Observations

Observations can be categorized as either systematic or nonsystematic observation (Salvia et al., 2013). Nonsystematic observations are also classified as information observations, which is when the observer simply watches an individual in his or her environment and takes notes on the behaviors, characteristics, and interactions of the student that seem significant (Salvia et al., 2013). During a systematic observation, the observer is looking for specific observable events that define the behavior in question. During systematic observations, the observer measures the frequency, duration, amplitude, and latency of each behavior (Salvia et al., 2013). Observations can provide powerful, detailed, and accurate information about the student being assessed and his or her surrounding environment, and what directly affects him or her.

Record Review

Student records contain important information including demographic information, previous test scores, attendance data, and school notes about the student's academic and behavioral performance, social skills, and academic achievement. Record reviews are important for teachers and testing evaluators to examine the past experiences of the student. Staff can find when problems first appeared for students, the severity, and the interventions used that were both successful and not. For students who have not had previous difficulty, record reviews can help show staff that the observed issues are new.

PURPOSE OF ASSESSMENT

To determine whether a child has a disability and is eligible for special education services, and to diagnose the specific nature of the student's problems or disability, assessments must be completed to determine the individual needs of the student. The assessments should cover all areas related to the suspected disability, including cognitive, social/emotional, speech and language, self-help, psychomotor, and vocational needs and abilities (Gargiulo & Bouck, 2018).

The evaluation team draws on the information gathered during the evaluation period, which is carefully considered and utilized in the eligibility determination. If it is determined that a child has a disability and needs special education and related services then an IEP must be developed to meet the student's individual needs (Gargiulo, 2016). Assessment information provides the detailed information needed to develop an IEP that is specific to the student in need. Specific information from the assessments helps the special education team determine what goals and benchmarks are necessary and drives educational decisions on behalf of the student identified (Gargiulo, 2016).

TYPES OF ASSESSMENTS

When a student is evaluated there are different assessments that can be completed to help the team assess the students suspected disability and needs. Students can be provided psychological assessments, which look at a student's cognitive abilities, social skills, behavior, and emotions. Educational evaluations focus on how the student performs on school-related academic tasks, and other related service provider assessments such as speech language, occupational therapy, or physical therapy could be included if it connected with the student's disability or suspected disability.

Psychological Assessments

Psychological assessments are powerful tools that help people understand a person's cognitive strengths and weaknesses. Modern intelligence tests were created to find a fair and accurate method of identifying children and adolescents who needed additional help in school (Binet & Simon, 1916). Intelligence tests can be long-term predictors of a wide variety of important life outcomes such as academic achievement, high school graduation, and income (Deary, Whiteman, Starr, Whalley, & Fox, 2004). Psychological assessments help professionals prioritize resources so that students who are most likely to fall behind can keep up and succeed.

Wechsler Intelligence Scale for Children

The Wechsler Intelligence Scale for Children (WISC) is the dominant clinical measure of intelligence used today and is currently in its fifth edition (Pearson Education, 2019). The WISC-V is a normed test appropriate for children and adolescents in the United States age 6:0–16:11 years (Pearson Education, 2019). The WISC was designed to identify intellectual giftedness, intellectual disability, specific cognitive strengths, and weakness for identification or diagnosis of specific learning disabilities in educational, clinical, and research settings (Flanagan & Alfonso, 2018). The assessment can be used in neuropsychological evaluations to help evaluate various aspects of neuropsychological functioning; yet, is typically used for the purpose of treatment planning and educational placement decisions (Flanagan & Alfonso, 2018).

The WISC-V has 21 subtests, five primary index scales, as well as five ancillary index scales and three complementary index scales (Pearson Education, 2019). The subtests can be combined in a variety of ways to estimate diverse aspects of cognitive functioning including verbal comprehension, visual spatial reasoning, fluid reasoning, working memory capacity, processing speed, general ability, and long-term storage and retrieval (Flanagan & Alfonso, 2018).

Wide Range Achievement Test

The Wide Range Achievement Test (WRAT) is an assessment that measures and monitors fundamental reading, spelling, and math skills (Flanagan & Alfonso, 2018). The assessment is appropriate for students ages five and older and helps identify students with possible learning disabilities (Flanagan & Alfonso, 2018). This assessment provides scoring and reporting for word reading, sentence comprehension, spelling, and math computations. Administrators do not need to complete the entire battery, as they are only able to administer the subtests that are needed by the students. The WRAT can also be provided in small group or individual testing situations (Flanagan & Alfonso, 2018).

Gray Oral Reading Test

The Gray Oral Reading Test (GORT), now in its fifth edition, is one of the most widely used measures of oral reading fluency and comprehension in the United States (Farrall, Wright, & Wright, 2018). This is a standardized norm-referenced assessment that can be used to diagnose a student with a reading disability, or to identify students who may need more intensive or explicit instruction in reading in order to make adequate progress (Farrall et al., 2018). The GORT can be administered individually for students ages 6 to 23:11. The GORT measures reading rate, accuracy, fluency, and comprehension. It also provides an Oral Reading Index, which is a combined measure of fluency and comprehension (Farrall et al., 2018).

Related Service Assessments

Related services help children with disabilities who would benefit from special education by providing extra support in specific areas of need. Related services can include speech language pathology, physical therapy, occupational therapy, audiology services, and medical services (Gargiulo, 2016). Evaluations must assess all areas related to a student's suspected disability and must identify all the of the special education and related service needs (Gargiulo, 2016).

Achenbach System of Empirically Based Assessment

The Achenbach System of Empirically Based Assessment (ASEBA) offers a comprehensive collection of questionnaires used to assess adaptive and maladaptive functioning (Farrall et al., 2018). This three-part assessment rates student behavior from three different viewpoints: the caregiver, the student, and the teacher (Farrall et al., 2018). ASEBA is for multiple age groups, including preschool, school-aged, adults, and older adults. It is widely used in mental health services, schools, medical settings, child guidance, training programs, and is available in over 100 languages. ASEBA attempts to capture the similarities or differences in behavior across settings and through interactions with different people (Farrall et al., 2018).

Behavior Assessment System for Children

The Behavior Assessment System for Children (BASC), third edition, includes a teacher, parent, and student self-rating scale, a structured developmental history, and a student observation system (Reynolds & Kamphaus, 2015). The BASC measures both clinical and adaptive dimensions of behavior and personality. The BASC-3 Behavioral and Emotional Screening System (BESS) can be used in a clinical or school setting and provides information on student behavioral and emotional functioning that identifies children and adolescents ages 3 to 18 (Reynolds & Kamphaus, 2015).

Behavior Rating Inventory of Executive Functioning

The Behavior Rating Inventory of Executive Functioning (BRIEF-2) assesses impairments of executive functioning for students ages five to 18 both in the school and home environments (Gioia, Isquith, Guy, & Kenworthy, 2018). The BRIEF-2 is useful for students with a variety of disabilities and provides parents and teachers a questionnaire that contains 86 questions that measure different aspects of executive functioning (Gioia et al., 2018). The test has eight clinical scales which include inhibit, shift, emotional control, initiate, working memory, plan and organize, organization of materials, and monitor (Gioia et al., 2018). The BRIEF-2 gives the evaluator a well-rounded idea of the behavior of the student being evaluated (Gioia et al., 2018).

Clinical Evaluation of Language Fundamentals

The Clinical Evaluation of Language Fundamentals (CELF-5) is an assessment that was designed to assess a student's language and communication skills in a variety of contexts, determine the presence of a language disorder, describe the nature of the language disorder, and plan for intervention and treatment (Leaders Project, 2014). The CELF-5 consists of 16 subtests, which includes an observational rating scale. The assessment should be administered as an independent test and it provides evaluators with a core language score, receptive language, expressive language, language structure, and language content standard scores (Leaders Project, 2014).

Test of Written Language

The Test of Written Language (TOWL), fourth edition, is a comprehensive diagnostic test of written expression that is used to identify students who have difficulty with writing, determine the student's specific needs, and documents the student's progress in writing (ProEd, 2009). The TOWL contains seven subtests, which are vocabulary, spelling, punctuation, logical sentences, sentence combining, contextual conventions, and story composition, which are combined together to form an overall writing composite score (ProEd, 2009).

Educational Assessments

Academic achievement tests are used to assess academic skills, which focus particularly on reading, writing, and math, and are used to diagnose academic learning disabilities as well as identify the academic strengths and weaknesses of an individual student (Braaten, 2018). Educational assessments compare a student's academic functioning with other students of the same age or grade. Within each of the main testing categories of reading, writing, and mathematics there are several subtests and educational assessments. In reading, for example, an educational assessment may look at basic reading skills such as letter identification and look at higher order thinking skills such as the inferential comprehension of a grade level passage (Braaten, 2018).

Woodcock-Johnson IV

The Woodcock-Johnson IV (WJ IV) is a broad-scope assessment that focuses on academic achievement, cognitive abilities, and oral language (Farrall et al., 2018). The system is organized into three independent, complementary batteries to include an achievement test, cognitive abilities test, and oral language test (Farrall et al., 2018). All tests can be used independently or as a combination. The WJ IV achievement test includes 20 subtests for measuring reading, mathematics, written language, and academic knowledge and is appropriate for children from ages of four to young adults 20:6 (Farrall et al., 2018). The WJ IV also provides diagnostic information as well as grade-level performances on discrete literacy and mathematical skills (Farrall et al., 2018).

FINAL THOUGHTS

Assessing a student for a disability is more than just a bird's-eye view of his or her abilities. The progression to special education requires a team of professionals to delve deep into student strengths and struggles to find the gaps in functional performance, behavioral expectations, and academic achievement and decide, based on clear data, if those gaps are due to a disability. The team is tasked with using academic and psychological assessments, observations, and record reviews to make those determinations. Using the Child Find Mandate within IDEA, educational teams meet, make decisions, and create IEPs to address student needs on an individual basis.

POINTS TO REMEMBER

- The Child Find Mandate of the IDEA requires states to find, locate, and evaluate all children from birth to age 21 who may have a disability and require special education services, including children who are highly mobile, homeless, migrant, or children who are wards of the state.

- Assessment in special education is the process used to determine a student's specific strengths and weaknesses and to determine if the student is eligible for special education services.
- The purpose of an assessment is to assist with the student's eligibility and disability diagnosis, IEP development, and guidelines to differentiated instruction.
- During the assessment process data should be collected from a variety of sources including observations, parent input, record reviews and tests that lead to a more complete picture of student strengths and struggles.

Chapter Four

Laying the Foundation for Success

Developing Meaningful Individualized Education Plans

Each child in public school who receives special education and/or related services must have an IEP. Every IEP must be individualized and be written to meet the student's specific needs (US Department of Education, 2010a). This legal document is the foundation of a quality education for children with disabilities and aims to improve educational results. The IEP process could be considered one of the most critical elements to ensure effective teaching, learning, and better results for all children with disabilities.

DEVELOPING MEASURABLE GOALS AND OBJECTIVES BASED ON PRESENT LEVELS OF PERFORMANCE

The IDEA requires every IEP to include a statement of present levels of academic achievement and functional performance. Academic achievement is performance in academic areas such as reading, writing, math, science, and history, and relates to the skills the student is expected to master (Center for Parent Information and Resources, 2017d). Functional performance is the context of routine activities that include everyday living such as social, behavioral, and mobility skills.

Specific and accurate information on current performance is essential. Generalization descriptions contribute nothing to the determination of a student's current level of achievement. When created correctly, the IEP will provide the information needed to determine the specific academic and functional needs to be addressed in the IEP goals. The present level of achievement is the basis for accommodations, supplementary aids and services, and program supports deemed appropriate by the team (Burton, 2018).

Goals must address the student's unique educational needs and be tightly aligned to the present level of performance in each area of need, and to the services (Burton, 2018). The components of current levels of performance include a description of the student's strengths specific to the knowledge and skills required to learn at grade level, a description of the student's needs (academic and functional) that should stipulate the skills required for the student to access and progress in the general education classroom, and the impact of the disability on the student's involvement and progress in the general education curriculum (Burton, 2018).

After obtaining accurate present levels of performance, annual goals and benchmarks can be created (Federation for Children with Special Needs, 2013). Annual goals are measurable statements that identify what knowledge, skills, or behaviors a student is expected to be able to demonstrate within a set period, beginning with the time the IEP is implemented until the next scheduled review (Center for Parent Information & Resources, 2017a). Annual goals are created to meet the student's needs as identified by the present level of performance. The IEP must list measurable annual goals consistent with the student's needs and abilities to be followed during the period beginning with placement and ending with the next scheduled review by the team.

The goals and objectives provide a system for determining if the student is progressing in the special education environment and general education classroom, and if the placement and services are appropriate to meet the child's identified educational needs (Cornell Law School, n.d.). A goal without a clear statement of a student's present level of performance and a specific objective against which the student's progress can be measured is not a measurable goal (Bateman & Herr, 2010).

The US Department of Education describes measurable goals and short-term objectives as critical to the strategic planning used to develop and implement the IEP for every child with a disability. Measurable annual goals set the general direction for instruction and assist in determining specific courses, experiences, and skills that a student will need to reach their vision. Using the acronym SMART (Bateman & Herr, 2010), IEP goals should be:

- **Specific:** Goals must have a corresponding measure in the present level of performance section in the IEP. Well-written goals make it clear on exactly what should be measured (Bateman & Herr, 2010).
- **Measurable:** A measurable goal allows the team to know what progress the student has made since the last measured performance. A well-written goal makes it clear on exactly what is being measured and how it is being achieved. A measurable goal should include:

- Observable learner performance which is the behavior the student is expected to do that is observable, visible, or countable.
- Actions such as label, write, draw, count, or read orally would be appropriate, while actions such as improving, knowing, or enjoying would not be observable, countable, or measurable behaviors.
- The conditions should include what the student will be provided, such as access to technology, a dictionary, or the use of a calculator.
- The specific level of the student's expected achievement includes information about the student's speed, accuracy, frequency, or quality of work.
- A goal must have specific criteria, so that the educator knows if the goal was reached. Objective criteria must include how much must be completed and how well it must be done to meet the goal. The addition of a percentage is not helpful when the IEP fails to define a starting point, ending point, or the curriculum and evaluation criteria that should be used (Bateman, 2010).

- **Achievable:** Focus on what tools, skills, and attitudes are needed to make this goal attainable. The goal should be a stretch for the student, but just far enough out of reach that it is possible. Making a goal that is too big will only lead to frustrations later on.
- **Relevant and Realistic:** Goals and objectives are individualized and address the student's unique needs that result from the student's disability. Goals are never based on district curriculum, state or district assessments, or other external standards. When creating goals, the team should always take consideration of the student's current level of performance to create realistic goals for the student to work toward.
- **Time Limited**: Including a time frame will provide the length of time that the student has to demonstrate a skill or behavior to show that the goal is achieved. This also enables the team to monitor progress at regular intervals.

Data Collection

Teachers need well-written goals to know what is being measured, how it is being measured, who is measuring it, and the frequency in order to keep appropriate data (Blerkom, 2017). If a goal is not written in measurable terms, the team will not keep appropriate and meaningful data to assist in making instruction-based decisions. Data collection for specific objectives should be taken by related service providers with expertise in the subject (ASHA, 2010). Speech pathologists, for example, would collect all language data for a student.

Technology has improved and has simplified data collection for educators. Electronic data collection of students' annual IEP goals is a practical solution to time and resource-intensive special education paperwork reduction and is efficient and effective (Gordillo & Miller, 2017). Using technology to collect data simplifies the process, provides data of trends for individual students and groups of students across multiple grades and schools, provides graphical representation of progress, and is easily understood for teachers, paraprofessionals, and parents (Gordillo & Miller, 2017).

Using Assessments to Drive Planning

Objective data from evaluations should be used to create meaningful IEPs. Assessment is the ongoing process used by qualified personnel to identify the student's unique strengths and weaknesses and the ways that the educators can appropriately meet the student's unique needs (Center for Parent Information and Resources, 2017a). No one discipline, or profession, possesses all the resources or clinical skills needed to construct the appropriate interventions and educational program for students with disabilities, a large number of whom have complex needs (Gargiulo, 2016).

Intellectual assessments provide information regarding the student's overall problem-solving ability with a specific focus on working memory, processing speed, and the student's ability to process visual-perceptual information versus verbal information (Holdnack, n.d.). If a battery of tests is used flexibly by a school psychologist, psychological assessments could help identify the specific areas of cognitive strengths and weakness that could be used to develop interventions to improve student success within the classroom.

Communication is assessed by SLPs. The assessments look at articulation, fluency, grammar, phonology, morphology, semantics, and pragmatics. SLPs provide valuable insight into how a communication disability should be managed, and what services and accommodations are critical to meet the student's individual needs (ASHA, 2010).

ALIGNING GOALS AND STATE STANDARDS

When implemented properly, a standards-based approach to developing IEPs blends the best of special education and standards-based education (Fitzpatrick, Hawboldt, Doyle, & Genge, 2015). All students, including students with an identified disability must be provided the opportunity to learn the general education curriculum surrounded by peers. Students receiving special education services have the right to be taught the same academic standards expected for all students, and all students should have access to the general education curriculum to allow them the opportunity to learn content-based, grade-level standards that can increase their readiness for college and a career (Dragoo, 2017). Standards-based IEPs provide this opportunity for students with disabilities.

A standards-based IEP is a process, and a document that is informed by and based on the state academic standards containing measurable annual goals developed by the team to meet the unique needs of individual students and facilitate the achievement of enrolled grade level academic standards (Virginia Department of Education, 2016). Standards-based IEPs are built on the belief that a student with a disability is capable of achieving grade-level proficiency if given the appropriate instruction and support and addresses a broader, more meaningful set of academic skills and knowledge than a traditional IEP (Project Success, 2017).

State standards define the knowledge and skills students should receive from the public school education in mathematics and language arts (Common Core State Standards Initiative, 2018). Standards provide statements of outcomes all learners should achieve and are typically arranged by grade level and content area. Standards are not curriculum, are not intended to define how teachers teach, and do not decide what services are provided. An important way that IEPs promote learning in the general curriculum is through alignment with state standards.

Alignment is the process of matching two educational components, which then strengthens the purpose and goals of both (Fitzpatrick et al., 2015). Alignment occurs when there is a match between the written, taught, and tested curriculum, and IEPs can be aligned with state standards to help align instruction with the general curriculum. IEPs that are aligned with the state standards can prepare students for state assessments (Courtade & Browder, 2016). Working on state standards prepares students to earn a high school diploma and succeed after graduation. Students at all levels receive tailored instruction and accommodations to help them achieve success in the general education.

When using traditional IEPs, educators sometimes teach students with more significant disabilities functional or life skills curriculum as a replacement for the general education content. Aligning an IEP to state standards can help the team select academic goals that are meaningful for the student and promote access to the general education curriculum (Courtade & Browder, 2016). All students with IEPs will be provided appropriate instructional adaptations either through accommodations or modifications based on their individual needs, which are documented on the IEP (Cortiella, 2008).

Standards-based IEPs include goals that promote learning in the state standards and provides goals for the strategies that students need to develop to learn the general education curriculum (Rohrer & Samson, 2014). Students with disabilities learn the same standards for their grade level placement. For the student to be successful, educators need to plan for the use of instructional supports, accommodations, and assistive technology (Brown-Chidsey & Bickford, 2016). Special education teachers need to become familiar with the state standards for each student's assigned grade level. Unpacking the skills that are embedded within each standard helps to identify access points for all levels of learners (Cortiella, 2008).

Standards-based IEPs encourage collaboration and awareness among the team of educators (National Center and State Collaborative, 2015). Special education teachers, general education teachers, and related service providers gain a better understanding of the state academic content standards and work together to support student learning. Although general education teachers are typically familiar with the state standards, this process will help them better understand what a student with a disability needs to achieve grade-level expectations.

A standards-based IEP for students with moderate and severe disabilities may have some goals that do not align with state standards, such as toileting independently, although some functional skills can be integrated into instruction in all classrooms during natural teaching moments (Cortiella, 2008). Many skills are taught to students that do not need to be put as IEP goals (National Center and State Collaborative, 2015). The goals should focus on skills that are aligned to standards that have the greatest impact across academic areas which will allow the student increased access to grade-level content.

Related service providers can also align to the standards by focusing on the specific skills that are limiting the student's access or progress in the general education setting. When creating goals that align to the standards for students with moderate and severe disabilities the team should select skills that promote overall English language arts and mathematical skills, focus on self-determination skills, use assistive technology to increase active and independent responding, and use real-life activities to give meaning to the academic concept (Courtade & Browder, 2016).

ACCOMMODATIONS AND MODIFICATIONS

Students with disabilities who receive special education services need accommodations or modifications to the general education curriculum to successfully participate (PACER Center, 2015a). Accommodations allow students to complete the same assignment or assessment as the other students with changes in the timing, formatting, setting, scheduling, response, or presentation. An accommodation does not alter what is being measured in a significant way (PACER Center, 2015a). A modification is an adjustment to an assessment or assignment that changes the standard or what is measured (PACER Center, 2015a).

Informed decision making for accommodations is critical for ensuring successful and meaningful participation for students with disabilities in the general curriculum, and district and state assessments. Evaluating how effective accommodations are should be an ongoing process, and teams should not assume that accommodation selection carries over from year to year (TN Department of Education, n.d.). To make effective decisions regarding a student's accommodations, the IEP team should gather and review information about the student's current level of academic performance, functional performance in relation to the general education curriculum, and which supports the student utilizes during instruction and assessments.

The IEP team including the student, when appropriate, should review the student's current accommodations, the effectiveness of each accommodation, and should discuss what accommodations and modifications are necessary; all decisions must be in accordance with the student's individual unique needs and written into the IEP. Accommodations are generally grouped into four categories to include presentation, response, setting, and timing (Vanderbilt University, 2018).

- Presentation accommodation might include providing students with audio books, large print, braille, or read aloud.
- Response accommodations might include allowing students to utilize technology, the use of a scribe, providing a graphic organizer, or word prediction.
- Setting accommodations include preferential seating, changes in the location of a classroom, and providing students with a study carrel.
- Timing accommodations include extended time, frequent breaks, and separating long testing into multiple testing sessions. (Vanderbilt University, 2018)

PROGRESS MONITORING

The IDEA envisioned a public school system fluent in prevention science, data collection, and progress monitoring in order to best improve outcomes for students with disabilities (Vannest, Burk, Payne, Davis, & Soares, 2011). A scientifically based practice is used to assess student academic progress and evaluate the effectiveness of instruction to improve student success; progress monitoring estimates the student's rate of improvement and identifies students who are not demonstrating adequate progress in order to alter instructional variables to better meet the needs of individual students (Vannest et al., 2011). Teachers should use progress monitoring to design more effective, individualized instructional programs for struggling learners.

The IEP should state how progress will be measured toward annual goals, and there should be a progress monitoring plan put in place. A progress monitoring plan should identify and define academic and functional (behavioral) knowledge as well as abilities and skills; determine how and when data will be collected and by whom; use interventions as a means to collect data as well as standardized testing over a set time frame; and evaluate all data points and information (Center for Parent Information & Resources, 2018).

Members of the team responsible for delivering instruction for IEP goals should be responsible for monitoring progress toward those goals; for example, if a student has a decoding goal that is serviced through the school's reading specialist, the reading specialist would be responsible for monitoring progress for that goal. Although paraprofessionals and teacher aides may assist in data collection for progress monitoring, the IEP team is responsible for determining if the child's progress is sufficient (Bryant et al., 2016).

Student learning can be measured using a number of methods. The methods are commonly grouped into two categories which are labeled as direct and indirect measures. The use of both direct and indirect measures when determining the degree of student learning that has taken place is recommended. Indirect measures are the perception, opinion, or attitude of the student or other person (Suskie, 2015). Indirect evidence is not sufficient by itself and must be mixed with direct measures. Indirect measures include rubrics, attainment scaling, and student self-monitoring.

Direct measures provide valid and reliable indications of student progress (Pennell, 2013). Direct evidence of student learning comes in the form of a student product or performance that can be evaluated. Direct measures can reveal what students have learned and to what degree. Since direct measures capture what students can actually do, they are considered the best measure of achievement levels of student learning on specific outcomes (Pennell, 2013). Behavior frequency recording, duration recording, interval recording, time sampling, tests, papers, and curriculum-based assessment are examples of direct measures.

Teacher observations provide valuable information for monitoring progress; however, they are subjective, and by themselves are not an adequate method of monitoring student progress in their areas of academic needs, particularly when a baseline has not been established (Pennell, 2013). A teacher's observations should be recorded in objective, nonjudgmental statements. Effective progress monitoring includes the measures of what is outlined in the IEP, an equivalent measure each time, regular and frequent data collection, strategies that are simple and quick to implement, and the ability to analyze performance over time (Bryant et al., 2016).

FINAL THOUGHTS

The IDEA requires that the child's progress be reported to parents at least every grading period (Center for Parent Information & Resources, 2018). Without objective, measurable, and measured objectives, this cannot be fulfilled. Progress monitoring helps IEP teams address any lack of expected progress toward annual goals and make decisions concerning the effectiveness of curriculum delivery (Center for Parent Information & Resources, 2018). SMART goals should be defined in the IEP and changes to instruction should be considered based on progress monitoring data. Progress monitoring is a vital component of an IEP and essential to the evaluation of the appropriateness of a child's progress. By implementing progress monitoring, IEP teams can ensure that the educational programming delivered for students with disabilities will be meaningful and beneficial.

POINTS TO REMEMBER

- Each child in public school who receives special education and related services must have an IEP, which is written to meet the student's specific needs.
- IEP goals should be SMART: specific, measurable, achievable, relevant and realistic, and time limited.
- Progress monitoring is a scientifically based practice used to assess student academic progress and evaluate the effectiveness of instruction to improve student success. Likewise, any lack of expected progress toward annual goals can be clearly observed and decisions concerning the effectiveness of curriculum delivery can be discussed.
- Accommodations and modifications can be made to the presentation, response, time, and setting of students' academic work to help them be more successful.

Chapter Five

Finding the Right Fit

The Least Restrictive Environment

The issue of appropriate placement for children with disabilities has generated considerable controversy and debate throughout history. Federal legislation mandates that services be provided to students in the LRE (Rothstein & Johnson, 2013). Students with disabilities should be educated in the setting that most closely approximates the general education classroom and yet still meets the student's unique needs. For a large number of students, this setting is in the general education classroom through inclusion.

Successful inclusion requires a new attitude or fresh thinking about where and how students with disabilities should be educated (Gargiulo & Bouck, 2018). A major problem faced by general education teachers as they work to become more inclusive in their practices of teaching is how to respond to and respect the individual differences of learners that include, rather than exclude, what is available in the regular education classroom (Florian, 2012).

Students with varying disabilities can be better involved in the general education class when given sufficient opportunities to actively participate, and when teachers positively identify and develop their capabilities. Skilled teachers must create and implement lessons that are meaningfully designed to accommodate all students and aid academic success (Florian, 2012). Classroom teachers can improve inclusion and the education of students with disabilities by utilizing the expertise of the special education teacher, differentiating instruction, utilizing universal design, and developing specifically designed instruction (Texas Education Agency, 2018).

DIFFERENTIATED INSTRUCTION FOR DIFFERENT LEARNING STYLES AND LEVELS

All students have individual learning preferences, backgrounds, and needs. Differentiated instruction (DI) is a student-centered approach that changes the pace, level, or type of instruction based on an individual learner's needs, styles, or interests (Tomlinson, 2014). Teachers can successfully differentiate district-mandated curriculum, state standards, or individual lessons; however, the biggest challenge is often in attempting to respond to an increasingly complex group of student needs, backgrounds, and learning styles (Tomlinson, 2014). Although most general education teachers recognize the contrasting learning needs of the students they serve, they often need support on how to plan and manage instruction that requires different students completing different activities (Celli & Young, 2014).

DI enhances learning for all students by engaging them in activities that better respond to their particular learning needs, strengths, and preferences. Differentiation is a two-step process where the teacher should first analyze the degree of challenge and variety in the current instructional plan and curriculum, while also being aware of the student's struggles and strengths (Sindelar et al., 2014). Teachers should be aware of students' unique learning styles to address individual differences (Celli & Young, 2014). The premise of DI is that students with disabilities can gain understanding of concepts when presented with multiple-instructional strategies that engage their learning strengths (Tucker, 2018).

In one three-year study in Canada, it was found that DI in K–12 French classrooms consistently led to positive results, especially when using small groups with targeted instruction for learning-disabled students (McQuarrie, McRae, & Stack-Cutler, 2008). Teachers indicated that DI resulted in improved classroom management and student learning (Tomlinson, 2014). DI supports students with learning disabilities by helping them retain content and skills, reducing time to absorb information, and allowing the learners the ability to demonstrate learning in a variety of ways (Tomlinson, 2014).

Students do not all learn the same way and therefore all students cannot be taught the same way. Teachers need to adjust their teaching style to reflect the needs of the students. Students may need a different level of support that can be determined through formative assessment. Differentiated classrooms reflect the teacher's thoughtful diagnosis of the students' learning needs and purposeful planning of activities and projects that address specific learning gaps (Tomlinson, 2014).

Elements of Curriculum That Can Be Differentiated

DI requires teachers to be flexible in their approaches to teaching and adjust the curriculum and presentation of information they use with the specific learners in the classroom, rather than expecting students to modify themselves for the curriculum (Dixon, Yssel, & McConnell, 2014). Teachers must recognize the students' varying background knowledge, readiness, language, and learning interests, and then execute on that awareness responsively in planning content, process, and final products (Dixon et al., 2014). Adjustments may occur in the content being studied, in the activities used to learn the content, or in the product completed to prove understanding of the content.

Content

Content is the information and ideas that students grapple with to reach the learning goals. Teachers achieve successful differentiation of instruction by varying the content in multiple ways, so students can access essential learning concepts.

Tiered Content

In tiered content, all students complete the same type of activity; however, the content varies by difficulty. Typically, students are divided into three groups based on readiness. The activities assigned to the low, middle, and high groups differ in terms of complexity.

Variety of Materials

Teachers can differentiate content by offering a variety of materials. Teachers can provide a range of textbooks, for example, which provides additional books above and below grade-level texts. Classrooms can also hold a variety of supplemental materials such as magazines, newspapers, audio books, games, or computer resources.

Process

How students take in and make sense of the content can be considered the process. Teachers teach the same concept or skill to each student in a way that makes sense of the topic or skill differently.

Learning Center

Centers can be an effective way for teachers to offer a range of activities that can target students' readiness levels, interests, or learning profiles. Centers contain activities for students to learn, practice, or build on a skill or concept.

Manipulatives

Providing students with concrete objects will help them to develop a conceptual understanding of a topic or skill; for example, students may use an abacus to count by fives, or colored blocks to find a pattern.

Product

An assessment of content; teachers provide students with a variety of ways to demonstrate their knowledge of a taught skill. Teachers provide clear expectations and a variety of options including visual, auditory, kinesthetic, analytic, creative, and practical options.

Examples

Some examples used in classrooms are diorama, poem, debate, travel brochure, written report, video, skit, play, PowerPoint presentation, poster, puppet show, essay, or painting.

Professionals in the field of education know that for instruction to be successful for students with disabilities, the general education and special education teachers need to collaborate to design and implement effective strategies (Deason, 2014). The concept of DI is based on the need for general education teachers to change instruction to meet the needs of diverse learners in the general education class, including students with disabilities. For inclusion to become successful, teachers and service providers must be willing to provide DI in schools and know how to implement it within their classrooms. Many general education teachers struggle with implementation of DI due to insufficient time for planning, time constraints, and resources (Deason, 2014).

Utilizing Universal Design for Learning

Another way to serve different students in the general education classroom is through a concept known as universal design for learning, commonly referred to as UDL (CAST, 2018). Although different, both DI and UDL recognize that each student's learning is unique. DI emphasizes the central role of the teacher to modify content and process in order to address the needs and learning styles of each child; while UDL emphasizes proactive design of the environment and curriculum (CAST, 2018; Tomlinson, 2014). Together, they can provide a powerful combination of strategies to reach the needs of all students as they work to successfully reach the goals of instruction.

UDL is a way to design curriculum that increases flexibility in teaching and decreases the barriers that frequently limit student access to materials and learning in the classrooms (Hall, Meyer, & Rose, 2012) Students are given equal access to learning, not simply equal access to information. It allows the students to determine the most appropriate method for assessing information while the teacher monitors the learning process (Hall et al., 2012). UDL guidelines provide suggestions based on research in the learning sciences for how to effectively design curriculum with flexible options that can support a student becoming an expert learner.

The research-based framework for designing curriculum involves educational goals, methods, materials, and assessments that enable all individuals to gain knowledge, skills, and enthusiasm for learning. The three UDL principles are to (1) to support recognition learning by providing multiple means of representation; that is, offer flexible ways to present what we teach and learn; (2) to support strategic learning by providing multiple means of action and expression for how students learn and express what they know; and (3) to support effective learning by providing multiple means of engagement, and flexible options for generating and sustaining motivation for the why of learning (CAST, 2018; Hall et al., 2012).

UDL encompasses education for all learners, which includes general and special education students and focuses on designing curriculum that provides fair access and opportunity to the same content in ways that works best for different students (Tomlinson, 2014). All curricula have four essential components to include goals, assessments, methods, and materials (Hall et al., 2012). Goals express a clear message that provide appropriate challenges for all learners and do not raise unintentional barriers in how they are articulated.

All assessments should include both formative and summative learning opportunities that are sufficiently flexible to provide accurate information on how well learners are meeting goals, and to inform adjustments in methods and materials to make instruction more effective (Tomlinson, 2014). Assessments can and should be designed to provide data to guide instructional activities and to assist individual learners (Tomlinson, 2014). Instructional methods and materials should be flexible and varied to provide the right balance of access, challenge, and support for learners, and allow learners to achieve their goals in ways that work best for each individual (Tomlinson, 2014).

EFFECTIVE COLLABORATION

The IDEA emphasizes the importance of providing access to the general education curriculum to students with disabilities, thus allowing them to meet the educational standards (Lee, 2018). Schools focus on inclusive models of education for students with disabilities that include higher expectations and increased teacher accountability, which requires effective collaboration and communication among the general education and special education teachers (Kauffman et al., 2017). Within an inclusion framework, both general education and special education teachers have the responsibility for the education of students with disabilities.

Effective teacher collaboration is defined as engaging in regular routines where teachers communicate about classroom experiences in an effort to strengthen pedagogical expertise and encourage each other to try new things (Gargiulo & Bouck, 2018). When educators work together, they form important professional and personal relationships. Teachers draw support from each other and delegate tasks which allow teachers to feel effective. Collaboration between teachers contributes to school improvement and student success (Sindelar et al., 2014).

Collaborative Consultation Model

Although there are many models available for teachers to follow for successful collaboration, one model is the Collaborative Consultation Model (Idol, Paolucci-Whitcomb, & Nevin, 1995). The collaborative model of consultation is a problem-centered approach that requires both the special education teacher, general education teacher, and other trained professionals such as school counselors, psychologists, administration, and speech language pathologists to develop creative and effective solutions for successful inclusion of students with disabilities within the general education classroom (Idol et al., 1995).

Essentially, there are two roles for this model to include the consultant and the consultee. The consultant is a trained professional such as a special education teacher, psychologist or occupational therapist with expertise in a specific area, and the consultee is a staff member, typically the general education teacher, who is responsible for carrying out the intervention (Idol et al., 1995).

The special education teacher primarily plays the role of the consultant; however, neither the special education teacher nor the general education teacher is an expert in this process because the role of expert shifts depending on the issue and conversation. Both the special education and general education teachers need support from each other for ideas that can best contribute to a positive solution (Kauffman et al., 2017). The general education teacher, for example, would be the expert during a conversation about grade-level curriculum, while the special education teacher would be the expert when collaborating about a student's difficult behavior.

Consultants lead the team in solving the learning and behavioral problems that are exhibited from students with disabilities in the general education setting. The consultant provides indirect services to the student by providing direct services to the consultee, who provides the direct support (Dettmer, Thurson, & Dyck, 2004). The consultant provides relevant information on intervention design, data collection, monitoring of skills, evaluation and continuous training of new skills. When collaborative consultation is working well, the consultant's role is a facilitator of the consultee's ideas (Kampwirth & Powers, 2015).

The special education teacher works as a member of the general education team to assist in the efforts to make decisions and execute a plan that will be in the best interest of the students. This involves the team engaging in regular face-to-face meetings so that the expertise may be shared (Kampwirth & Powers, 2015). This helps to develop the collaborative relationship among staff. Consultation within the classroom can involve classroom observations, data collection, or the special education teacher modeling effective strategies and implementation of new interventions (Kampwirth & Powers, 2015).

Consultation outside of the classroom can include discussions of a student's IEP, reviewing data, modifying materials, reviewing current research, or discussing challenges and developing interventions for specific students (Kampwirth & Powers, 2015). The benefits of collaborative consultation between the special education and general education staff is that the appropriate students remain in the LRE and utilize the expertise of both the general education and special education teachers (Kampwirth & Powers, 2015).

Throughout the model there is increased communication among staff with the result of sharing knowledge, experiences, materials, resources, and the shared responsibility for the education of specific students. With the increase of collaboration, students receive the attention and focus of multiple instructional perspectives and enhanced skills and attitudes (Dettmer et al., 2004).

Essential skills for a successful collaborative consultation model include a relationship based on mutual respect and trust, strong interpersonal communication skills, ability to receive constructive criticism and suggestions, openness to try new instructional techniques and methods, willingness to find time to support changes, and weekly time devoted to consultation.

Cooperative Teaching Model

Cooperative teaching, or co-teaching, has become increasingly popular for meeting inclusion mandates (Gargiulo & Metcalf, 2013). Co-teaching is an instructional delivery model used to successfully teach students with disabilities within the LRE, which is the general education classroom. The general education and special education teachers share the responsibility of planning, delivering, and evaluating instruction for all students (Smith, Polloway, Doughty, Patton, & Dowdy, 2015).

The goal of co-teaching is to create options for learning and provide supports for all students in the general education classroom, including students with disabilities, by combining the context expertise of the general education teacher with the pedagogical skills of the special education teacher (Smith et al., 2012). Using this model, the general education teacher is typically viewed as the master of content while the special education teacher is considered the master at providing appropriate accommodations and modifications to allow students access to the general education curriculum (Sindelar et al., 2014).

It is vital that the educators plan together and switch roles to eliminate one teacher feeling like an assistant, or not feeling valued at all. There are many approaches to co-teaching and a variety of arrangements can be used throughout the day depending on the specific classroom circumstances. The strategy that a team chooses often depends on the needs and characteristics of the students, curricular demands, amount of professional experience, the educators' relationship, teacher preference, and the amount of space available (Gargiulo, 2016).

Co-teaching can involve teachers functioning in many different positions throughout the day. During the one teach/one observe method, one teacher presents the classroom instruction to the entire class while the second teacher conducts other tasks such as gathering data on specific students, a small group of students, or identifying issues (Sindelar et al., 2014). This method allows the observing teacher to provide feedback on what activities and contents were the most effective, which allows for reflective practice.

Teachers can also have one teacher take the lead and provide the classroom instruction, while the other teacher provides support and individual assistance to individual students or small groups (Sindelar et al., 2014). Station teaching is when a lesson is divided into two or more sections and presented in different locations throughout the classroom (Smith et al., 2012). One teacher presents one section of the lesson to half of the class, while the other teacher provides the other section of the lesson to the other half of the class, and then the groups rotate. Station teaching is effective at all grade levels.

Alternative teaching places one educator with large group instruction, while the other teacher provides small group instruction (Gargiulo, 2016). This can be used for remediation purposes or enrichment activities. The most successful method of co-teaching will need to be evaluated by the teachers based on the students in the classroom and the best method may change throughout the school day.

DEVELOPING SPECIFICALLY DESIGNED INSTRUCTION

Specifically designed instruction as defined by IDEA regulations refers to adaptations to the content, methodology, or delivery of instruction that addresses the unique needs of a child that results from the child's disability, ensures access to the general education curriculum so that the child can meet the educational standards that apply to all children, and are guaranteed by the IDEA and implemented in accordance with the individual educational plan process (Rothstein & Johnson, 2013).

Specifically designed instruction should ensure access to the general education curriculum through modifications so that the student can meet the same academic standards as their general education peers (Gargiulo & Bouck, 2018). This, in turn, should guarantee progress toward meeting IEP goals and objectives. Specifically designed instruction means organized and planned instructional activities that are provided by a special education professional to modify, as appropriate, the content, methodology, or delivery of instruction (Hall, Quinn, & Gollnick, 2018).

What makes instruction individualized for a student with a disability and different from what the general education students receive is how the instruction is linked to the student's IEP goals and objectives. Specifically designed instruction is a systematic and intentional process that specifically addresses the student's needs as expressed in the IEP goals and objectives (Hall et al., 2018). When the content is modified, students with disabilities are learning different skills and knowledge than typically developing same-aged peers (Hall et al., 2018). All students are working toward the same standard, such as reading, but may be working on a different skill and standards indicator.

Students who receive significant special education services may receive instruction in skills that are not a component of the general education curriculum; rather, it may be a part of the student's IEP goals and objectives (Gargiulo & Bouck, 2018). Specifically designed instruction integrated into the core instruction, supplemental intervention, and intensive intervention will look different for every student with a disability (Gargiulo & Bouck, 2018). This unique set of supports is provided to each student based on their learning needs to remove barriers that result from the student's disability. The supports are reflected in the student's IEP and are infused throughout the student's learning experiences and environments as described in the IEP (Florida Department of Education, 2015).

Tiered Supports

Tier 1 supports are provided to all students by the general education teacher in collaboration with school-based team members to assist students in the mastery of the standards and the prevention of skill gaps to ensure career and college readiness (Hall et al., 2018). Instruction and supports are designed and differentiated for all students in all settings to ensure mastery of the standards and universal instructional goals.

Tier 2 supports are provided by the general education teachers in collaboration with the support of school-based team members who have content knowledge and intervention expertise (Hall et al., 2018). For students who need supplemental supports to master their standards, greater targeted and focused interventions and supplemental supports are aligned with standards and universal instructional goals.

The most intense intervention based on individual student needs are provided in Tier 3 and aligned with universal curriculum, instruction, and supplemental supports (Hall et al., 2018). This includes reduced group sizes, explicit and systematic instruction, and frequent progress monitoring and services provided by the general education teachers, special education teachers, and related service providers that have deep content knowledge and expertise implementing evidence-based interventions.

LEVELING COURSEWORK

There are several methods to differentiate instruction to meet the needs of all students. One strategy to reach all students' varying abilities and accommodate learning styles that teachers can use is tiered assignments, which can be used within flexible groups. Tiered assignments are assignments designed at different levels of complexity according to students (Tomlinson, 2014). Tiered assignments can allow all students to focus on essential understandings and skills but work at different levels.

Tiered assignments allow teachers to start students where they are academically and ensures that each student is appropriately challenged and come away with the skills necessary for success (Tomlinson, 2014). Tiered assignments allow students various ways to arrive at an understanding based on interest, readiness, or learning profiles, and assists teachers in meeting the needs of students with varying abilities, learning styles, and interests. Assignments can be tiered by complexity, resources, outcomes, the process, and the product.

Classroom material cannot be successfully tiered without having student assessments to guide your decisions on how students should be grouped, and which tiers should be created (Hall et al., 2018). The first step to creating tiered activities is to provide students with a preassessment of the material. The preassessment helps the teacher determine what tiers are necessary and which students should be included within each tier.

One common way to tier a lesson or activity is by the student's ability level. For this to be successful, teachers need a concrete understanding of the student's abilities around the lesson and create tiers to meet those needs and abilities (Loveless, 2013). Many examples of tiered lessons based on readiness have three tiers to include below grade level, at grade level, and above grade level (Loveless, 2013). The number and level of tiers is based on student assessment and the range of abilities within the classroom.

Tier 1 is for students who do not have the appropriate background knowledge or skills to be independently successful. Tier 1 requires a significant amount of teacher support. Tier 2 is for students who have an understanding of the material, and Tier 3 is for students who can work primarily independently, who have shown mastery of the skill through preassessment, and need to be challenged with more in-depth and complex activities (Loveless, 2013).

DIFFERENTIATING INSTRUCTION WHILE MEETING GRADE-LEVEL EXPECTATIONS

Students with disabilities are entitled to appropriate accommodations that allow them to fully participate in state- and district-wide testing. The determination of necessary accommodations or modifications is part of the development of the IEP and decided based on the student's individual needs. The IEP team should consider the student's learning strengths, difficulties, how the student's disability affects the achievement of the grade-level standards, and the level of specialized instruction the student requires to meet grade level standards (Center for Parent Information & Resources, 2017e).

A review of the accommodations that the student is currently utilizing should be examined and modified as needed. Assessments can be individualized by making changes to the presentation, response, and timing (Center for Parent Information & Resources, 2017e). Making accommodations to the presentation can allow students to access information in ways that do not require them to visually read standard print, using other learning styles and senses such as auditory, multisensory, tactile, and visual (Celli & Young, 2014; University of Kansas: School of Education, 2018b). Assessments can offer large text, human read aloud or text to speech, audio tapes, magnification devices, or talking materials such as clocks, timers, and calculators (Celli & Young, 2014).

Students may be allowed to complete activities, assignments, and assessments in different ways using an assistive device or organizer. Items such as a human scribe (or speech-to-text software), graphic organizer, respond on the testing booklet rather than carry the material over to another document, or utilize a tape recorder are all ways for students to receive the accommodations they need (Morin, 2018c). Students who have a difficult time remaining concentrated for extended periods, or have a health-related disability, may require extended time, frequent breaks, or multiple testing sessions (Morin, 2018c).

FINAL THOUGHTS

The LRE offers students with disabilities the opportunity to work alongside their nondisabled peers in academic settings that best match their needs. At times this is an inclusion setting, while other times students need to be in a different location where their more extensive needs can be met with success. As inclusion becomes the norm, general education teachers must be taught best practices in reaching these struggling students. Seeking the assistance of special education teachers, utilizing universal design for learning, understanding students' personal learning styles, differentiating instruction, and specifically designing instruction are ways in which general education teachers can become special education experts within their own classroom; thus, meeting the needs of their students on IEPs.

POINTS TO REMEMBER

- All students have individual learning preferences, backgrounds, and needs. It is the goal of the educator to find each student's preferred style and gear teaching to that strength. This means using differentiation so that all students are represented in the learning process.
- Classroom teachers can improve inclusion and the education of students with disabilities by utilizing the expertise of the special education teacher, differentiating instruction, utilizing universal design, and developing specifically designed instruction.
- All students should be in the LRE to the maximum extent possible.
- Specifically designed instruction ensures access to the general education curriculum through modifications so that the student can meet the same academic standards as their general education peers.
- Collaboration between general education and special education teachers contributes to school improvement and student success.

Chapter Six

Understanding the Role of the Paraprofessional

Leveraging Student Success

Paraprofessionals are essential members of the special education classroom, providing support services to students with a wide range of disabilities. According to the US Bureau of Labor Statistics (2018), as of 2016 there were 1,308,100 paraprofessional jobs available in the United States. That number is expected to increase by 8% over the next 10 years (US Bureau of Labor Statistics, 2018). Of these 1.3 million jobs, most consist of spending considerable time working closely with students who have severe disabilities (Brock & Carter, 2015b). Part of the job performed by paraprofessionals requires them to provide instructional, behavioral, and emotional support to disabled students.

Interestingly, most paraprofessionals are not required to have an education beyond a high school diploma to carry out their jobs, although some districts require an associate degree (Brock & Carter, 2015b; Conley, Gould, & Levine, 2010). It is surprising, however, that many paraprofessionals report receiving little to no in-service training on how to best perform their jobs (Brock & Carter, 2015a; Brock & Carter, 2015b; Garwood, van Loan, & Gessler Werts, 2018). As more and more teachers and parents request paraprofessional support within the classrooms, it is crucial to understand the best ways in which to utilize educational assistants in order to provide more effective programming for students with disabilities.

CHALLENGES TO THE ROLE OF PARAPROFESSIONAL

Generally speaking, a paraprofessional (also known as an instructional assistant or paraeducator) works under the guidance of a licensed teacher who supervises the support given to one or more students (US Bureau of Labor Statistics, 2018). Most paraprofessionals are tasked with providing direct support to students with a range of disabilities, although some paraprofessionals work in inclusion classrooms and support all students.

Some of the duties performed by paraprofessionals may also include assisting the teacher with grading and assessing students, providing school-wide supervision of students, and helping to enforce behavioral expectations in the classroom (US Bureau of Labor Statistics, 2018). Paraprofessionals assigned to the neediest students may also be required to help with diapering, feeding, and other day-to-day tasks (ASHA, 1999).

At times there may be an overreliance on the paraprofessional, creating challenges within the educational setting. One such difficulty is the reliance on the paraprofessional to provide direct instruction and modifications for students. Although the paraprofessional's role is to assist with service delivery in the classroom, they are to do so under the supervision of a licensed teacher (McGrath, Johns, & Mathur, 2010).

Due to resources being stretched so thin in the world of special education, paraprofessionals often assume the role of a secondary teacher, making curricular decisions for students, which is outside their purview (McGrath et al., 2010). This becomes especially problematic when students with disabilities receive the bulk of their instruction from paraprofessionals, while students without disabilities receive their instruction from a certified teacher (Breton, 2010).

Another challenge faced by paraprofessionals is a lack of training and preparation. Although paraprofessionals are visible in more classrooms than ever before, just their mere physical presence is certainly not enough to improve social and academic outcomes for students with disabilities (Brock & Carter, 2015a). Special education teachers often become the de facto trainers of the paraprofessionals with whom they work. Many special educators themselves are untrained to provide the types of ongoing supervision and training necessary to increase the effectiveness of their instructional assistants (McGrath et al., 2010). Many paraprofessionals report wanting more training and professional development opportunities, yet there is a lack of options, and professional development is often not without its flaws (Brock & Carter, 2015b).

One of the major challenges with professional development opportunities for both teachers and paraprofessionals is that they are often presented in a one-time format, which very rarely encourages generalization to other settings (Brock & Carter, 2015b; Stockall 2014). Studies have shown that these types of workshops have an extremely limited impact on helping the paraprofessional to gain any meaningful skills that they can then use in everyday practice (Barnes, Dunning, & Rehfeldt, 2011; Brock & Carter, 2015b; Hall Grundon, Pope, & Romero, 2010). Additionally, these types of seminars rarely encourage follow-up training, and so they provide the false sense of having mastered a skill when in reality more support and training is needed (Hall et al., 2010).

It is also important to keep in mind that paraprofessionals do not have the same educational requirements as other support personnel, posing additional challenges. As inclusion has become the standard of special education, paraprofessionals have been charged with gaining more qualifications for working with students with special needs; for example, Maine rates paraprofessionals on three different levels according to educational background (Brenton, 2010).

Level I paraprofessionals hold a high school diploma or equivalency, while Level III paraprofessionals have completed a minimum of 90 credits of approved study in a field relevant to their practice (Breton, 2010). The majority of paraeducators have not completed college, nor have they gained related experience in a related field (US Bureau of Labor Statistics, 2018). This can be especially challenging for paraprofessionals whose role is to support students with severe learning and emotional disabilities.

When paraprofessionals are tasked with providing substantial support to both students and teachers, but with little training, job burnout is highly probable. This is especially noticeable in substantially separate classrooms where students remain for the bulk of the day. Paraprofessionals who have the role of supporting in a 1:1 setting, especially with students who have emotional and behavioral needs, often report that they feel depressed, exhausted, and underappreciated (Garwood et al., 2018).

The unfortunate side effect to the stressors placed on instructional assistants is an inability to provide effective support to the student, resulting in little to no gains on IEP goals (Garwood et al., 2018). Little research has been done on the physical and emotional needs of paraprofessionals in this role (Ansley, Houchins, & Varjas, 2016). It is crucial, therefore, for teachers and school administrators to provide effective training and support mechanisms for all paraprofessionals.

PARAPROFESSIONAL QUALIFICATIONS: A BRIEF LOOK AT THE HISTORICAL CONTEXT

To begin to understand how to effectively train and work with paraprofessionals as co-educators within the classroom, it is important to look at the history of the profession. Paraprofessionals were not always as highly relied upon for instructional support as they are today. In fact, many paraprofessionals began as parents who sought out part-time work once their children reached an age of increased independence (Conley et al., 2010). Soon laws were passed that tightened down on educational requirements in schools, and school districts looked to the paraprofessional to provide increasing amounts of support to both students and teachers (Conley et al., 2010).

Beginning with the ESEA of 1965, President Johnson's "War on Poverty" focused on increasing the amount of funding to public schools in which the population of students came from low-income families (Paul, 2016). The rationale behind the creation of ESEA was that equal access to quality education was one of the most important ways to ensure that students remained in school; therefore, increasing their chances of breaking free from the cycle of poverty (Paul, 2016).

Title I of the act emphasized closing the gaps in math, writing, and reading skills for students from low-income and middle-class families. As a result, more funding would be given to schools to increase instructional support personnel; however, in the beginning stages of ESEA, schools would often recruit parents from local neighborhoods who had various backgrounds and skills to fill these support positions (Conley et al., 2010). Many of these support personnel would be charged with small tasks such as making copies or supervising the lunchroom (Conley et al., 2010).

Fast forward to the enactment of Public Law 94-142, otherwise known as the Education for All Handicapped Children Act (EAHCA) in 1975, paraprofessionals were assigned to provide for students' basic needs (Conley et al., 2010). At that point, there was some questioning surrounding whether students with severe disabilities could even be educated, and so schools moved to utilize paraprofessionals who were much less expensive to employ than teachers (Giangreco, Smith, & Pinckney, 2006). The need for increasingly skilled support personnel was becoming evident as students with more intensive needs began to be included in the general population of the school.

With the passage of the No Child Left Behind Act (NCLB) in 2001, students were required to pass standardized exams that proved their proficiency on state educational standards (Paul, 2016). Teachers were now required to be highly qualified to teach in their chosen field; however, paraprofessionals were still not required to have any additional training beyond passing a basic competency exam (Conley et al., 2010).

Most recently, the ESSA of 2015 ensures that all teachers and principals are evaluated and supported to increase accountability in all school districts, particularly those that are underperforming (Paul, 2016). Yet, while paraprofessionals must also undergo performance evaluations, there doesn't appear to be a clear consensus in all states on the best ways in which to prepare and train paraprofessionals for the increased responsibilities of their roles (Brock & Carter, 2015b). Some paraprofessionals are trained on the job while they are working with students, while others are sent to outside professional development seminars that may or may not be geared toward the unique needs of the paraeducator (Brock & Carter, 2015b; Garwood et al., 2018).

WORKING EFFECTIVELY WITH PARAPROFESSIONALS: GUIDELINES FOR A COLLABORATIVE ATMOSPHERE

Paraprofessionals are valued and necessary in the world of special education. It is important to create a collaborative working environment in which the instructional assistant feels as though he or she is being included in the instructional planning and intervention for the students with which he or she works. Many special educators report difficulties finding the most effective ways of accomplishing this task (McGrath et al., 2010).

While the working relationship between teacher and paraprofessional is supposed to be collaborative, the fact is that the teacher is essentially the paraprofessional's supervisor. In most instances, the teacher, in conjunction with the principal, is responsible for completing the paraprofessional's performance review (McGrath et al., 2010). This can create tension within the relationship, especially if the teacher is younger than the paraprofessional or if the teacher is new to the building (McGrath et al., 2010).

One method that can assist in overcoming these types of challenges is creating an environment in which communication is both expected and valued. Clear communication is key in any working relationship, but particularly in a relationship that requires rapid decision-making (Stockall, 2014). When working with students with disabilities, one cannot use a one-size-fits-all approach to teaching. Similarly, teachers should not expect paraprofessionals to adhere to directives handed down at the beginning of the day without continuous communication and evaluation from the classroom teacher (Stockall, 2014).

As much as educators communicate with students throughout the day, communicating with other adults who work in the classroom can be challenging, especially when there is a disagreement. Ivey, Ivey, Zalaquett, and Quirk (2012) suggest that clear communication consists of seven skills that must be practiced ensuring effective delivery.

Listening

Listening means giving full attention to the other person and fully focusing on the message he or she is trying to convey (Stovall, 2014). Listening on the part of both parties is the basis of effective communication and is essential to encouraging active and meaningful participation in discussions. Although the teacher oversees the planning, and therefore is responsible for the educational outcomes of the students, he or she needs the support of the paraprofessional so that effective instruction can take place (McGrath et al., 2010; Stovall, 2014). Teachers must show the paraprofessional that their knowledge is important and valued.

Utilize Open-Ended Questions

While "yes" or "no" questions have their place when looking for quick answers, open-ended questions require individuals to elaborate on a given topic. When teachers engage with their instructional assistants on the topic of how to best support students, it is critical that the teacher makes every effort to gain a wide range of information from the paraprofessional (Stovall, 2014). It is especially important to ask questions that allow the paraprofessional to showcase his or her expertise. For example, a new teacher may benefit from hearing what tricks have been effective for a paraprofessional who has previously worked with a group of students. These suggestions may be helpful in planning how to best approach instructional planning.

Utilize Closed Questions

It would seem obvious to say that asking questions before making assumptions is the best way to avoid misunderstanding and frustration for both the teacher and paraprofessional; however, in the world of education, where decisions are often made in a moment's notice, basic communication often gets missed. Although it is a better idea to ask questions that will create the framework for thoughtful discussion, there are times when asking simple "yes" or "no" questions is appropriate and necessary.

Gaining quick answers to questions can bring insight to the teacher with regard to how best to work with the paraprofessional (Stockall, 2014). This requires little analysis on the teacher's part, while gauging the effectiveness of the working relationship with the paraprofessional. Simply asking the paraprofessional whether or not he or she has had training in a specific area, for example, is much more effective than delegating a task to him or her for which there has been no preparation. Asking the questions ahead of time can save both teacher and paraprofessional from unnecessary stress in the future.

Clarifying Information

Because of the nature of working with children who have intensive needs, it is often challenging for the adults working with these children to always react with a clear head. Oftentimes paraprofessionals who have had inconsistent training aren't experienced enough to recognize alternative methods of handling problem behavior or learning challenges. This can create tension between the teacher and paraprofessional, especially if the teacher hasn't had the opportunity to guide the paraprofessional toward the most effective way of working with a student.

Stockall (2014) argues that it is crucial for teachers to ask clarifying questions that help them to understand the paraprofessional's viewpoint; for example, when a student continuously exhibits behavioral challenges within the classroom, it becomes very taxing on the adults with whom the student is working. The trained teacher has strategies to assist in working with the student or, at the very least, understands how to disengage with the student so as not to feed into the problem behavior. A paraprofessional, however, who has not had training in this area can often become frustrated and overwhelmed and may resort to either using a disciplinarian model or attempting to befriend the student in hopes of changing the behavior.

For teachers working in this situation, it can be very stressful, and the teacher may feel undermined by the paraprofessional. Merely asking the paraprofessional why he or she acted a certain way with a student is unlikely to shed much light on the true challenges that the paraprofessional is having in his or her job. Stockall (2014) suggests that teachers should ask specific questions that help them to understand how to best support the paraprofessional. An example would be asking the paraprofessional to explain the specific behaviors of the student that are most frustrating, and why he or she is having a hard time disengaging from confrontation. Simply issuing directives to the paraprofessional will do little to solve the problem and will likely continue to exacerbate the strain on the adult/student relationships within the classroom.

Paraphrase What Was Said

One of the biggest pitfalls to working with another adult in the classroom is that oftentimes words and signals are misinterpreted (Stockall, 2014). Effective communication can only be accomplished when each adult has a clear understanding of what the other is trying to convey. This can be achieved by simply rephrasing what was said to ensure that the other's viewpoint is understood. For example, saying, "What I hear you saying is that you are more concerned with the student's behavior than his academic capabilities," can help to clarify the main concern and, therefore, help to create dialogue surrounding effective interventions.

Acknowledge the Paraprofessional's Message

Looking the speaker in the eye and acknowledging his or her opinions and concerns is key to creating an effective working relationship. Being dismissive of the experiences that the paraprofessional brings to his or her position is not only bad for communication but can also create unnecessary tension that can be palpable to the students. While the teacher oversees the everyday planning for the classroom, the execution of the lessons and interventions could not take place effectively without the assistance of the paraprofessional. Asking for the paraprofessional's opinion encourages collaboration, which, in turn, creates a more positive and productive working relationship.

Provide Reflective Feedback

Just as it is necessary to provide feedback to students suggesting ways in which to improve their work, so too it is important to provide feedback to the paraprofessional suggesting ways in which to improve his or her practice (Stockall, 2014). As previously stated, many paraprofessionals lack proper training, which can subsequently create challenges for the teacher, paraprofessional, and students (Brock & Carter, 2015b). The teacher oversees the daily workings of the classroom and, as such, part of his or her responsibility is to provide useful feedback to the paraprofessional.

Having a consultation block wherein the teacher and paraprofessional reflect on the day's challenges, providing the teacher the opportunity to share strategies with the paraprofessional is optimal. This can also be accomplished in a side-by-side coaching model in which the paraprofessional receives individual instruction with an experienced teacher while he or she is engaged in practice (Montana Office of Public Instruction, 2017).

BALANCING THE NEED FOR PARAPROFESSIONALS: SUPPORT VERSUS OVERRELIANCE

It is not surprising that requests for paraprofessional support are on the rise (Garwood et al., 2018; Giangreco, Doyle, & Suter, 2012). Schools often cite understaffing as one of the key reasons that students lack the support they require (Giangreco et al., 2012). Due to budgetary reasons, hiring more licensed teachers is often not feasible; thus, schools look to paraprofessionals to provide much needed support within classrooms. Studies suggest that, despite the belief that paraprofessionals are severely needed to help support students, there have been few positive outcomes reported (Stockall, 2014).

Students who have substantial paraprofessional support often report feeling stigmatized by their peer group (Giangreco, Suter, & Hurley, 2011; Stockall, 2014). Additionally, the lack of preparation provided to paraprofessionals often interferes with their ability to provide quality support to the students for whom they are responsible, especially in the area of instruction (Stockall, 2014).

Yet, teachers report the exact opposite when asked about the helpfulness of having a paraprofessional in the room. The support that paraprofessionals are perceived to provide is often cited as having a positive impact on the job satisfaction and stress levels of the teachers (Giangreco et al., 2012). The role of the paraprofessional is designed to provide support to the teacher in order to increase student outcomes, not to provide respite to teachers who may feel overworked or unsupported themselves (Breton, 2010; Giangreco et al., 2012; McGrath et al., 2010; Stockall, 2014).

It is important to keep in mind that paraprofessionals are, indeed, valued members of the educational community; however, it is up to schools to determine the best ways in which to utilize the skills and talents these individuals bring to the classroom. Perhaps, due to a misunderstanding on the part of both parents and schools, paraprofessionals should not be the first support mechanism proposed for students with disabilities (Giangreco et al., 2012). With the need to adhere to LRE, paraprofessionals are often thought of as the first support service to help disabled students navigate the general education classroom. Giangreco and colleagues (2012) argue, however, that the need for better, more inclusive teaching practices is warranted far more than adding an extra adult into a classroom.

Diversifying teaching practices is the answer to eliminating the increased need for paraprofessional support. While it is true that there will always be students who need more intensive supports than others, there is nothing about paraprofessional support that is more effective than other combinations of supports when tried over a period of time (Giangreco & Broer, 2007; Giangreco et al., 2012). In fact, other less restrictive supports may prove to be helpful for students with social challenges; specifically, due to the need for these students to work with peer groups instead of being ostracized with an adult.

In all instances where intensive paraprofessional support is provided to a student, measures must be taken to continuously evaluate the paraprofessional's effectiveness and begin to fade supports as much and as soon as possible (Giangreco et al., 2012). There seems to be a myth that one-to-one support is meant to continue for as long as the child is in school; however, research has shown that fading supports and educating students on which strategies work best in helping them access their education works far better for long-term outcomes (Conley et al., 2010; Garwood et al., 2018; Giangreco et al., 2011; Giangreco et al., 2012; Stockall, 2014).

FINAL THOUGHTS

With the needs of students increasing at exponential rates, it is not surprising that school districts look to paraprofessionals to help provide support to both teachers and students. The lack of preparation and training options, however, coupled with the overreliance on paraprofessionals to support students for extended periods, often leads to burnout, job dissatisfaction and, in many cases, decreased support services for students.

Care must be taken not to overextend paraprofessionals in their duties. Expecting more than what they can physically, emotionally, and legally provide is a recipe for disaster. Teachers must focus on developing positive working relationships with the paraprofessionals in their classroom through increased communication and collaboration. When paraprofessionals are adequately supported, they are better able to carry out their own roles as support personnel, and as a result, they will positively impact the learning outcomes for students with disabilities.

POINTS TO REMEMBER

- Paraprofessional jobs are expected to increase substantially over the next 10 years as more students require assistance as identified in the IEP process.
- There are many challenges faced by paraprofessionals, including being expected to provide instruction and modifications to students without having the proper training and educational background to do so.
- Clear communication and expectations are key to developing an effective teacher- paraprofessional relationship.
- Decisions surrounding adding paraprofessional support should be made on the ability of the paraprofessional to be a true support, rather than just another adult in the classroom.

Chapter Seven

It's Not All About Academics

Addressing Disability-Related Behavior Problems and Social Deficits

Students with disabilities often need support in the areas of behavior and social skill development; however, all students require guidance in how to navigate social norms, especially when it comes to understanding what is acceptable or not acceptable in a school or community setting. Schools that are successful in handling the social and behavioral challenges of all students often show the best academic outcomes (Shuster et al., 2017). Conversely, schools that fail to employ structured programs for increasing appropriate behaviors are difficult places in which to teach children.

Schools are often inconsistent with the practices they adopt, often leaving the teachers in the building to haphazardly attempt to find a discipline protocol that works best for their classrooms. These discipline practices cannot often be generalized across school settings and are difficult to implement with fidelity (Shuster et al., 2017). When discipling students with disabilities, there are a multitude of factors that must be considered, not the least of which is the possibility of litigation that can stem from failing to follow proper due process procedures in disciplinary actions (Katsiyannis, Losinski, & Prince, 2012). It is crucial for special education teachers to have working knowledge of the discipline procedures for students with disabilities, as well as the ways in which to provide positive behavior supports to encourage more appropriate behaviors across settings.

THE LEGALITIES OF DISCIPLINE: THE CREATION OF THE MANIFESTATION DETERMINATION REVIEW

Several laws have been put into place to prevent students with disabilities from being unfairly removed from their educational setting based on behavior that may not be within their control. According to the IDEA (2004), before a school district can discipline a student for a period of time of 10 days or more, the district must first determine whether or not the behavior is a manifestation of the student's disability. This requires schools to hold a manifestation determination review (MDR) to ensure that students with disabilities that may impact behavior are not removed from their educational placement (Lewis, 2017).

Prior to IDEA, there was no discipline provision included in the law (Lewis, 2017). Under the EAHCA of 1975, lawmakers created provisions for ensuring that students with disabilities were not excluded from school altogether, that they were provided with adequate services, and that they were identified for potential underlying disabilities that may interfere with their access to education (Lewis, 2017).

Discipline procedures stemmed from individual cases that made their way to the courts. In the case of *Goss v Lopez* of 1975 (Swem, 2017), the court determined that all students who were subject to disciplinary action by the school should be afforded due process under the Fourteenth Amendment. This ensured that some kind of hearing was to take place before a student could be removed from his or her educational placement; however, school districts were not required to make a determination about the disability's impact on the student's behavior (Lewis, 2017).

In two later cases, one of which made its way to the Supreme Court, it was ruled that students with disabilities, particularly those who were labeled "emotionally disturbed," could be protected from disciplinary procedures, provided their behavior was substantially connected to the behavior infraction in question (Leagle, 2017; Wrightslaw, 2011). This would force school districts to keep the student in his or her agreed upon educational placement under the stay-put provision of the EAHCA.

Schools were granted the ability to remove a disabled child to an alternative educational placement if both the parent and district came to an agreement about the appropriateness of the student's placement (Walker & Brigham, 2017). Conversely, if the parent and school could not agree, then the school could request an injunction from the court to force the student into an alternative placement for the safety of the students and staff within the school (Wrightslaw, 2011).

As the IDEA went through reauthorizations, so too did the criteria for a manifestation determination review. Schools were at first charged with the task of proving that a student's disability did not impact the behavior; however, that requirement was changed to the standard of today, which requires the review team to answer two questions to include (1) Was the conduct in question caused by, or had a substantial relationship to, the child's disability?; and (2) Was the conduct in question the direct result of the school's failure to implement the IEP? (Katsiyannis et al., 2012; Walker & Brigham, 2017).

The review team is required to consist of relevant members of the student's IEP team, the parents, and representatives from the school (IDEA, 2004). Depending upon the team member's point of view, the results of the MDR can be skewed based on a number of factors, including personal opinions of the student, lack of information about the student's disability and/or historical background and, in some cases, coercion from other team members who have an interest in removing the child from his or her classroom (Katsiyannis et al., 2012; Walker & Brigham, 2017). Parents do have the right to appeal the decision to the school's designated hearing officer but, again, this process is also very subjective (Lewis, 2017).

On a positive note, students who are removed from their educational placement due to behavioral challenges are guaranteed educational services that are in line with their IEP goals and services (IDEA, 2004). Additionally, for behaviors that are found to be caused by the student's disability, schools are required to conduct a FBA and create a BIP to mitigate further behavioral infractions (Cheney & Jewell, 2012; Lewis, 2017).

Recognizing Disability-Related Behavior: When Is It a Manifestation?

Due to the subjectivity of the MDR, it is necessary to understand some of the guidelines by which teams are required to consider when looking at the possibility of a manifestation. Information from multiple sources should be examined by review team members in order to make the most educated and fair decision. Teams are required to examine the student's behavioral history, understanding of the behavior, and the behavior's relationship to the disability (Lewis, 2017). The following list has been adapted from Lewis (2017) in which a table suggests ways to make a determination of connection to disability.

Behavioral History

It's not likely a manifestation when:

- No recent behavioral problems.
- Previous behavioral challenges have not included assault.
- Concerns addressed in the IEP focus on verbal and not physical aggression.

- The team concludes that this behavior is atypical for the student.

It is likely a manifestation when:

- There is a history of aggression and anger from the student.
- The student lacks proper judgment or social skills.
- The student has been known to make poor social choices.
- The student has a history of noncompliance, and verbal and physical aggression.
- There is an FBA/BIP already in place that addresses the previously listed concerns.

Understanding of Behavior

It is not likely a manifestation when:

- The student engaged in the behavior so that his or her placement could be changed (e.g., a day off from school due to suspension).
- The behavior was planned and deliberate.
- The student is fully aware of the consequences of the action in question.
- The student can control his or her behavior.

It is likely a manifestation when:

- The behavior is impulsive and lacks control.
- The student doesn't understand the seriousness of the action.
- The student doesn't or can't think through the consequences.
- The student has difficulty controlling his or her behavior in unstructured environments.
- The student's behavior is inconsistent.

Relationship to Disability

It is not likely a manifestation when:

- The IEP team decides the behavior had no connection to the disability and was spontaneous in nature.
- The disability does not make the child prone to fighting.
- The disability is not characteristic of an impulsivity disorder.
- The student's disability is for an academic issue (e.g., specific learning disability in reading).

It is likely a manifestation when:

- The disability limits the student's alertness or awareness.
- The student has difficulty maintaining positive relationships with peers and staff.
- The student does not possess age-appropriate social or communication skills.
- The student's diagnosis of ADHD is characteristic of impulsivity and poor judgment.
- The student has a physical or cognitive disability that limits his or her ability to fully understand rules.

This is not an exhaustive list of considerations; rather, it provides a framework for thinking about a disability's influence on behavior. There are other considerations that may be taken depending upon the individual student's case (Knudsen & Bethune, 2018). The suggestions listed here demonstrate the breadth of possibilities that can influence the outcome of the decision-making process.

FUNCTIONAL BEHAVIORAL ANALYSIS AND BEHAVIORAL INTERVENTION PLANS

As stated in the latest iteration of the IDEA (2004), students whose behaviors are a result of their disability are required to be assessed for the function of their behavior. FBAs are tools that provide behavior support teams with information that can help to develop a clear plan of action for improving a student's challenging behaviors (Cheney & Jewell, 2012). The FBA is designed to allow the examiner to identify the likely reasoning behind the behavior's manifestation. A young student who continually runs out of the classroom at the beginning of a lesson, for example, may be using this behavior to avoid a nonpreferred task.

Examiners performing FBAs must look closely at the environmental factors influencing the behavior in question (Cheney & Jewell, 2012). After identifying the problematic behavior, examiners will look at the antecedent leading up the behavior. Once that is determined and tracked over a period of time, examiners can make a hypothesis about the likely function of the behavior (Cheney & Jewell, 2012). There are times when a student's behavior appears to have no observable relationship to an environmental stimulus. Students with mental health challenges or emotional impairments can often exhibit behaviors that appear to have no connection with an antecedent (Scott & Cooper, 2017).

For students with autism, behaviors that cannot be easily observed in conjunction with their antecedent often have more complex internal causes that are not easily observable (Scott & Cooper, 2017). An example might be a student who exhibits a sharp behavioral change after a slight change in routine. What would outwardly appear non-concerning to the person observing the behavior can have a severe impact on the child's ability to cope. Students who lack coping strategies are far more likely to act out as a method of taking control of an unpredictable situation (Scott & Cooper, 2017).

Completing the FBA leads into creating a BIP that includes supports and interventions that can help discourage or stop problematic behavior (Cheney & Jewell, 2012; Collins & Zirkel, 106). BIPs are meant to be individualized to each student's needs. Generally, the BIP is created by the person who completed the FBA and then disseminated to the rest of the staff with whom the student works. The BIP is designed to provide faculty with strategies for improving a student's behavior, as well as providing interventions and methods for both short and long-term reinforcement (Cheney & Jewell, 2012; Shuster et al., 2017).

While any staff member who is trained in completing FBAs can do so, many times this task falls to the board-certified behavior analyst (BCBA) or board-certified assistant behavior analysts (BCaBAs). BCBAs and BCaBAs help staff gain a deeper understanding of the student's behavior as their role is to evaluate programming and develop behavior plans for students in all educational settings (Kelly & Tincani, 2013). They are tasked with helping educators and other service providers with understanding the ways in which to utilize behavior modification strategies in order to help students with behavioral challenges develop more appropriate responses to stressors in their environment (Kelly & Tincani, 2013). Behavior analysts work collaboratively with educational staff to help plan appropriate interventions that will remedy the problem behavior (Smith, 2012).

POSITIVE BEHAVIORAL INTERVENTIONS AND SUPPORTS: USING POSITIVE INTERVENTIONS TO CHANGE NEGATIVE BEHAVIORS

PBIS is a mandate handed down from the 1997 reauthorization of IDEA (Positive Behavioral Interventions & Supports, 2018b). The provision states that schools are to use more positive interventions and supports rather than punitive measures to help change students' problematic behavior (Cheney & Jewell, 2012). As a result, more and more schools began to develop social skills programming and behavioral instruction that slowly became effective in dealing with challenging behavior. One of the problems with PBIS, however, is that it is rarely used for students with disabilities (Shuster et al., 2017). While a large number of schools, approximately 21,000, have put PBIS practices into place, not everyone benefits from the program (Horner & Sugai, 2015).

The goal of PBIS is to provide schools with a framework for creating an appropriate social culture within the school, while at the same time providing individual behavioral supports to those students who need them in order to achieve increased academic success (Horner et al., 2014; Shuster et al., 2017). The PBIS system consists of three tiers, and students are placed into a tier depending on level of need; however, it is not a stagnant system. Cheney and Jewell (2012) explain that each tier corresponds with the intensity of support and is much like the RTI model.

Tier 1: Intervention for All Students

During the Tier 1 phase, schools begin with developing a team of individuals who will be responsible for developing and refining the practices that will be used in the school-wide intervention system (Cheney & Jewell, 2012). Goals will be developed that focus on when and where students will be expected to participate in PBIS, as well as objectives identifying the priority of outcomes (Positive Behavioral Interventions & Supports, 2018b). As an example, schools may decide to focus on respect of all staff and students as one of its objectives. The staff would then teach the students about respect and create practices that model the ways in which to be respectful to others.

Using the PBIS guidelines, staff, students, and parents are taught to use the same language surrounding appropriate behavior so that these behaviors can be generalized across settings (Cheney & Jewell, 2012). The goal is that the Tier 1 supports will help school staff to develop responsive and positive relationships with all students (Stanton-Chapman, Walker, Voorhees, & Snell, 2016). At this level, schools collect data and then use that data to inform the decision-making committee on how to modify plans to best suit the needs of the students (Positive Behavioral Interventions & Supports, 2018b).

For the majority of the student population, Tier 1 supports are effective in replacing inappropriate behaviors with more acceptable behaviors; however, for approximately 20% of the student population, Tier 1 supports are not intensive enough for their level of need and educators and administrators look to level two supports in this instance (Shuster et al., 2017).

Tier 2: Supports on a More Individualized Level

Tier 2 supports are provided to students who have difficulty following the Tier 1 expectations. In order to identify students who may benefit from this level of support, staff may use behavioral screenings that take into consideration a child's number of office referrals or behavioral incidents within the classroom (Cheney & Jewell, 2012). Tier 2 interventions use intentional and individualized teaching methods to promote students' understanding of social and behavioral appropriateness (Stanton-Chapman et al., 2016).

For Tier 2 to be successful, staff must follow six guidelines: (1) there must be similar implementation for all students within the tier, (2) interventions must be readily available and easily accessible, (3) most staff must be included in the process, (4) there must be consistency with the Tier 1 expectations, (5) staff must monitor the students for progress, and (6) staff must incorporate functional assessments into the process (Hawken, Adolphson, MacLeod, & Schumann, 2009).

Tier 2 supports have been shown to be about 70% effective over an eight-week period. Cheney and Jewell (2012) cite several studies conducted over a five-year period wherein samples of students demonstrated a reduction in the amount of office referrals they received over the course of 12 weeks. While these interventions do not provide immediate relief from behavioral disruptions, when used consistently they certainly lessen the severity (Cheney & Jewell, 2012).

Tier 3: Intensive Support

Tier 3 supports are appropriate for only a small percentage of students, about 5% or less (Cheney & Jewell, 2012). This level of support is the most individualized and intensive of the three tiers, and involves regular FBAs, the creation of a BIP, and individualized assessments and interventions that are often tied to a student's IEP (Collins & Zirkel, 2016). Students with Tier 3 supports are often the most behaviorally challenged, displaying chronic behavior problems that often interfere with access to social and academic inclusion (Scott & Cooper, 2017; Stanton-Chapman et al., 2016).

It is especially important to use a wide range of evidence-based interventions within Tier 3. For students with emotional behavioral disorders, interventions such as peer-tutoring, cooperative learning, self-evaluation, modeling, and token systems have shown promise in helping to reduce behavioral outbursts at this level (Cheney & Jewell, 2012). The effectiveness of Tier 3 interventions is predicated on the FBA and BIP. Because so few students require this level of support, teams can truly focus on the individual student and really drill down the types of interventions that make the most sense.

For students with disabilities, the interventions are linked to the goals within the IEP and are monitored by the special education team; however, Tier 3 interventions do not always indicate that the student receives special education services. In fact, research suggests that many of the PBIS systems fail to include the special education population (Shuster et al., 2017).

Positive Behavioral Intervention and Supports and Special Education: Remaining Challenges to Behavior Intervention

Oftentimes the students with the most needs, such as students with emotional impairments and other mental health challenges, are the least likely to be included in the PBIS system (Shuster et al., 2017). There are many reasons for this lack of inclusion, the most impactful being a lack of training and access to supports for the special education teachers (Tillery, Varjas, Meyers, & Collins, 2010).

Many administrators and general education teachers believe that special educators already provide behavior intervention within their classroom and so do not need to be a part of the school-wide initiative (Shuster et al., 2017). This becomes problematic for a child who is designated as a special education student but receives all his or her instruction in the general education classroom.

With the move toward inclusion and least-restrictive environment, it is poor practice not to recognize that students of all backgrounds and disabilities can and should be included within the general population. That is not to say that there aren't students who will require intensive, individual instruction and support; however, this should be more of the exception than the rule (Shuster et al., 2017).

Much can be learned from including students with disabilities in the school-wide PBIS system as the nature of special education requires teachers to think outside the box to discover creative ways to solve problems; thus, these educators can be essential in helping to craft behavioral interventions that can be applied to the entire student population (Schuster et al., 2017). As the success of PBIS depends on the input and support of all stakeholders, it would make sense to include the individuals who have the most experience in working with behaviorally challenged students, such as special educators, school psychologists, and behavior professionals (Shuster et al., 2017).

FINAL THOUGHTS

When disciplining students with disabilities, school officials often walk a fine line between protecting the students and staff and protecting the school from litigation. With the creation of regulations surrounding disciplinary procedures for students whose behavior may be impacted by their disability, schools must be more cautious of how they approach suspensions and other removals. Procedurally, the IDEA provides clarity on the steps to follow to ensure a student is given due process. However, the actual process of identifying whether or not a student's disability impacted his or her behavior is ambiguous. School staff must remain as objective as possible when reviewing each individual case to ensure that the student has been provided with the fairest consequences based on the disability and behavior.

FBAs and BIPs can help staff to further understand the ways in which the disability is impacting the student's behavior, as well as the function behind the behavior (Collins & Zirkel, 2016). As a matter of fact, schools are required to conduct an FBA if the student's behavior is a direct result of his or her disability. Yet, many schools do not proactively turn to these assessments to help provide insight into a child's behavior until after something serious occurs. It would make sense for schools to seek the help of BCBAs and other behavior professionals to assist with planning for more positive behavior supports. This is especially important with the move toward including PBIS programs in schools.

While PBIS shows promising results for most students, there is little research into its effects on special education students at the school-wide level. Special education teachers most likely include PBIS systems within their classroom to address individual behaviors, but studies suggest that special education students and teachers are not consistently included in the school-wide PBIS process and in some instances, they are excluded all together (Horner & Sugai, 2015; Shuster et al., 2017; Tillery et al., 2010).

POINTS TO REMEMBER

- Schools that are successful in handling the social and behavioral challenges of all students often show the best academic outcomes.
- When discipling students with disabilities, there are a multitude of factors which must be considered, not the least of which is the possibility of litigation that can stem from failing to follow proper due process procedures in disciplinary actions.
- According to the IDEA (2004), before a school district can discipline a student for a period of time of 10 days or more, the district must first determine whether or not the behavior is a manifestation of the student's disability
- The MDR process is very subjective and can be difficult when team members are influenced by their personal opinions of the student.
- Students whose behavior is a manifestation of their disability are required to be assessed using an FBA.
- FBAs and BIPs allow teams to uncover the root of the behavior and then plan effective intervention to address it.
- PBIS is a system of interventions and supports that can be helpful for increasing positive behavioral outcomes for all students, yet students with disabilities are often excluded from school-wide initiatives.

Chapter Eight

Expanding the Team

Effective Collaboration with Outside Services and Professionals

Decisions surrounding changing a disabled student's education plan are made by a team of people who all have equal decision-making power; however, at times not all stakeholders are on the same page insofar as what the child requires to be successful (Ruppar & Gaffney, 2011). This can be especially stressful when team members cannot come to an agreement in the best interest of the student. IEP team meetings can be contentious and uncomfortable, putting the family and school district in a precarious position as they each use their expertise on the child to determine the most appropriate course of action.

As stated in the law under IDEA (2004), parents can bring individuals to team meetings who have knowledge of the child and his or her needs to include related service personnel such as outside therapists, as well as educational advocates (Burke & Goldman, 2017). Including individuals outside of the school setting can be both beneficial and challenging for school staff.

Outside service providers can often make suggestions about the student using a different lens; thus, educators are armed with fresh strategies to use with the student. On the other hand, there are times when outside providers can prove to be adversarial with the school staff, which can often create a tense relationship between the school and the family (Burke & Goldman, 2017). Understanding the roles of the most commonly included service providers can help educators gain insight into how to establish a mutually respectful working relationship that will result in the best outcomes for the student.

ADVOCATES

Oftentimes parents have difficulties navigating the special education system alone. Some reasons behind this include a lack of understanding of the technical terminology, feeling intimidated by the school, and an overall lack of knowledge of procedure (Burke & Goldman, 2017). This can create the feeling that schools are trying to take advantage of parents, or don't want them to enact their decision-making power as members of the team.

Because parents want the most beneficial services for their child, advocates are often hired by the parents to help them navigate the complexities of the special education process; however, the expertise of advocates can vary greatly. There is currently no formal process by which advocates can become certified (Burke & Goldman, 2017). Advocates can be anyone who has a vested interest in the child and who has a basic knowledge of special education, from former special education teachers to parents with disabled children who have had to navigate the system for their own child.

Although some advocates may be attorneys, most advocates are not lawyers and cannot serve as legal support in lieu of an attorney (Heitin, 2013). Many advocates are paid by the family, but some advocates volunteer their time to help families in need. One of the major challenges to working with advocates is that oftentimes these individuals use intimidation tactics to coerce the school into providing the student with services (Kirkland & Bauer, 2016). This can be especially stressful for new educators who have never worked with advocates and who may fear legal repercussions from disagreeing with the advocate's demands.

The role of the advocate is to support the family, and there can be dissension between the advocate and the school when both parties disagree on services; however, an advocate is one member of the team. All members of the team have equal decision-making power, although not all team members share the same expected outcome (Ruppar & Gaffney, 2011). Some paid advocates have an interest in retaining their clientele, and to do that they must be needed.

If a school finds a student ineligible for services, there is arguably no need for the family to continue with advocacy. This often leads advocates to push for additional testing or threaten schools with litigation in order to remain gainfully employed. In fact, research has shown that the introduction of an advocate into the team meeting impacts the decision-making process whereby team members often make a particular decision to avoid confrontation with the advocate (Kirkland & Bauer, 2016).

Facing an argumentative advocate can be unnerving for all team members; however, these suggestions, adapted from Heitin (2013), should serve to help create an effective relationship with an advocate.

- **Stay off the defensive:** Parents can legally bring anyone to a team meeting that they choose. When teams see an advocate, they often become defensive, ready to fight on behalf of the school. Heitin (2013) suggests that this is counterproductive to the needs of the child. Keeping in mind that the child's needs are at the heart of the meeting will help keep everyone focused and level-headed.
- **All advocates differ:** As previously stated, there is no licensing board for advocates and that proves problematic, especially when parents hire advocates that have little knowledge of school-based provisions; however, instead of dreading the interaction, educators should use this as an opportunity to make sure they are well-prepared for the meeting, including carefully reviewing the student's file, brushing up on the law, and perhaps even calling the parent to vet the concerns ahead of the meeting.
- **Not all advocates are confrontational:** Although the advocate's job is to stand up for the child's needs, not every advocate wants an argument. Services for a student are required to be considered irrespective of the needs of the school. Henceforth, the advocate may disagree or remind the parents of their rights. However, this does not mean they are looking for an argument with team members.
- **Details matter:** It may often feel like advocates are hyper-focused on every small detail within the student's IEP. Too often, schools create IEPs that are vague, with little attention to individualization. A good advocate who knows what to look for will often challenge the school on smaller details in order to ensure the child is getting all services and accommodations that he or she needs to be successful.
- **Some advocates are more knowledgeable than schools believe:** Good advocates have a solid working knowledge of special education law. Oftentimes school administrators are not as well-versed in the nuances of the rights of students with disabilities. However, if team members are open to constructive discussion, it is possible to create an appropriate plan for the student without unnecessary frustration.
- **Sometimes schools appreciate advocates:** Advocates who want what is best for the child will always advise the parent on what is needed for the child to be successful. If that means the child truly doesn't qualify for services, then the advocate will be straightforward with the parent. This can allow the school some respite from parents who continue to make demands or threaten litigation on school staff.
- **Advocacy services are more important now than ever before:** With the increase in students qualifying for special education services, there is a need for parents to be educated about their child's rights. Advocates can provide that assistance to parents who may be wary of the school system. Schools can often be reluctant to suggest services that will tax their rapid-

ly decreasing budgets, and so it is crucial that parents understand the services to which their child is entitled.

The most important point to remember when working with an advocate is that school staff have unique expertise regarding the child under the advocate's representation. Each team member brings a perspective unique to that individual, and just because team members disagree on issues, it does not mean that one person is right while the others are wrong. The lesson to take away from working with advocates is that the student's family wants what is best for their child, and so the more the school can work to educate, empower, and truly listen to the parent, the less likely confrontation will occur (Burke & Goldman, 2017).

EDUCATIONAL SURROGATES

Although most students have parents who will advocate for their needs, a small percentage of students have been appointed educational surrogates who will make educational decisions on the child's behalf. There are three conditions under which a surrogate parent may be appointed: (1) the parent is unknown or unavailable, (2) the student is a ward of the state, or (3) the parent requests a surrogate parent in writing (PACER Center, 2015b). Students in foster care may or may not have an educational surrogate depending upon whether or not the foster parent has been granted the legal signing rights over the child's educational decisions.

Educational surrogate parents are only appointed when a child has or is suspected of having a disability (PACER Center, 2015b; Special Education Surrogate Parent Program [SESPP], 2015). The educational surrogate's role does not extend beyond the decision-making process. For all other decisions related to a child's medical, therapeutic, or residential needs, the child welfare program of the respective state oversees those decisions.

In Massachusetts, for example, the Department of Children and Families (DCF) oversees all legal decisions for the children placed into their custody (Massachusetts Department of Elementary and Secondary Education, 2015). Consultation between the educational surrogate and DCF worker can take place; however, it is not within the scope of duties that are assigned to the educational surrogate to make decisions beyond school-based services and supports (Massachusetts Department of Elementary and Secondary Education, 2015).

Although it would seem as if the educational surrogate has a limited role in the child's life, these individuals fulfill very specific requirements that are critical to educational planning for a child with a disability. According to the

Special Education Surrogate Parent Program (2015) in Massachusetts, educational surrogates' responsibilities include:

- Accessing all of the student's educational records, including progress reports and report cards.
- Providing written permission for any and all special education evaluations.
- Reviewing all evaluations and attending all special education team meetings.
- Requesting special education team meetings when there are concerns surrounding the student's progress in school.
- Observing the student within the school setting to determine the appropriateness of placement.
- Signing rights on all IEPs, which includes the ability to accept or reject the proposed IEP.
- Filing complaints against the school if it is deemed that the school has violated the student's special education rights.

The educational surrogate parent is not likely to have intimate knowledge of the child beyond what he or she has reviewed insofar as school records; therefore, it is important for school districts to collaborate with the educational surrogate to ensure that he or she has the most comprehensive information to make the most informed decisions (PACER Center, 2015b).

Educators who have had negative experiences with advocates may be reluctant to collaborate with educational surrogates for fear of similar intimidation and confrontation. Educators should understand that educational surrogates are not the same as advocates; when an educational surrogate attends a team meeting, he or she has legitimate legal authority over the educational decisions being made for the child, whereas the advocate is a consultant to the family and has no legal authority to make decisions for the child (Kirkland & Bauer, 2016; Massachusetts Department of Elementary and Secondary Education, 2015).

One final note about children in foster care bears mentioning. Each year, there are approximately 800,000 children in the care of child welfare agencies (Zetlin, MacLeod, & Kimm, 2012). Although some children in foster care have an educational surrogate, the majority do not. The foster care system is complex and often involves children moving from district to district. Unfortunately, it is this lack of stability that often causes these children to fall through the cracks, leaving them vulnerable to failure and the possibility of dropping out of school altogether.

Children in foster care are often disproportionately identified as having disabilities (Zetlin et al., 2012). For the children who have been identified as needing special education services, oftentimes schools are not informed right away when a foster child enters the district. This creates a lapse in services, which negatively impacts the student (Zetlin et al., 2012). Keeping these challenges in mind can help educators to understand the struggles faced by these children and will allow them to make decisions that will create beneficial educational experiences for students at the highest risk.

COMMUNITY-BASED MENTAL HEALTH PROVIDERS AND THERAPISTS

Sometimes students with disabilities need services that must be provided beyond the school setting. There are several outside agencies that work collaboratively with schools to provide a continuum of therapy. Community mental health (CMH) therapists continue to play an important role in assisting autistic children and their families to find and receive appropriate behavioral and mental health treatment (Brookman-Frazee, Taylor, & Garland, 2010).

Many children with disabilities, especially those with autism spectrum disorder, also have co-morbid disorders that need treatment, ranging from anxiety disorders to schizophrenia (Mattila et al., 2010). This type of treatment cannot easily be provided by school-based therapists who lack clinical training; thus, CMH therapists can assist in developing treatment plans that can be shared with the school to help with the incorporation of strategies that will allow for the easier management of symptoms from co-occurring disorders (Brookman-Frazee et al., 2010).

CMH therapists face substantial challenges in providing effective treatment to children with disabilities; however, in many cases, CMH therapists themselves lack training in specific disabilities (Brookman-Frazee et al., 2010). Coupled with the brevity with which many of these practitioners see these patients, it becomes difficult to see improvements in patient outcomes (Brookman-Frazee et al., 2010). Additionally, it often takes a substantial amount of time to receive CMH services due to an already overloaded system, and so children who desperately need therapeutic intervention face long wait times to receive assistance (Brookman-Frazee et al., 2010).

Once those services are approved and rendered, it often takes a longer time to see results, which can further frustrate both families and educators. It is for this reason that it is critical for CMH services to collaborate with schools to ensure that a continuum of services is in place for the students receiving assistance from these agencies.

COLLABORATION STRATEGIES FOR SERVICE PROVIDERS

To ensure maximum benefit to students with disabilities, collaboration between service providers and educators must occur (Friend & Cook, 2013; Hart Barnett & O'Shaughnessy, 2015). Developing effective communication skills is the first step in ensuring that successful collaboration is taking place. Educators and service providers must actively listen to each other's perspectives and appreciate the levels of experience and knowledge each practitioner brings to the table.

Being that educators work with their students for approximately 30 hours per week, and outside service providers may only see the same students for one to two hours per week or when an IEP meeting is scheduled, it is important to understand that each professional has unique knowledge that is critical to developing a well-rounded plan of intervention (Hart Barnett & O'Shaughnessy, 2015). Respect for each professional's perspective is the best way to facilitate the most effective plan of action for students with disabilities.

Collaboration should be encouraged between teachers and outside service providers as well. Community providers can help with the implementation and sustainability of effective educational strategies for students with disabilities, especially for students with emotional disorders (Brookman-Frazee et al., 2010; Mattila et al., 2010; Shuster et al., 2017). Many schools have adopted the practice of allowing outside therapists to see their clients at the school as a way to make it easier for students in need to receive a continuum of services without the added stress of finding additional time and transportation. Community providers should be regarded as essential members of the student's team and should be incorporated to the largest extent possible into collaborative meetings and planning times, if applicable.

FINAL THOUGHTS

It is important to remember that decisions surrounding the planning for students with disabilities are made by members of a team. Although parents can bring anyone they choose to a team meeting, no one person has more decision-making power than another (Ruppar & Gaffney, 2011). There are several outside service providers who may participate in the team meeting, not all of whom may be willing to collaborate productively with the school, yet it is necessary to remember that each team member brings a unique perspective to the table. At the end of the day, everyone on the team is fighting for what's best for the student.

When parents are uneducated about the special education process or feel as though the school doesn't want to work with them, they may hire an advocate to help guide them through the process. Because working with advocates can be contentious, school staff could do more to explain special education processes to parents, be more transparent with the inner workings of the evaluation process, and provide in-depth explanations regarding how and why a child would or would not qualify (Burke & Goldman, 2017; Kirkland & Bauer, 2016). When parents feel supported by the school, they are less likely to require outside representation.

Similarly, when working with educational surrogates, child welfare agencies, or outside mental health therapists, school staff must be willing to encourage collaboration. For students who do not have parents to advocate on their behalf, educational surrogates take on that roll and ensure the student is receiving the most appropriate services (Heitin, 2013). It is important to keep in mind that educational surrogates and child social workers do not have intimate knowledge of the child, so many of their recommendations are based upon objective review of the student's case (Massachusetts Department of Elementary and Secondary Education, 2015). School staff need to work collaboratively with these individuals to ensure a clear understanding of the child's needs. Sharing relevant information with these providers is crucial for safeguarding against missed services and opportunities that will benefit the child.

POINTS TO REMEMBER

- Decisions around changing a disabled student's education plan are made by a team of people who all have equal decision-making power.
- IDEA (2004) states that parents can bring any individual they choose to team meetings.
- When parents feel as though they do not understand the special education process or feel as though the school is trying to take advantage of them, they may hire an advocate to help them through the process.
- Educational surrogates are not advocates; rather, they are appointed by the court to make educational decisions for a student with special education services.
- Community mental health therapists (CMHT) often work with disabled students to provide wrap-around services in conjunction with the supports provided by the school.
- Collaboration with outside providers is crucial for ensuring the most appropriate and well-rounded plan of intervention.

Chapter Nine

Harnessing the Home-School Connections

Planning for Effective Parent-Teacher Partnerships

Working collaboratively with the parents of a disabled student is necessary for providing the best educational outcomes for the student. It is not surprising that schools have become more transparent with their methods and interventions, and many are striving to create open relationships with outside service providers (Magaldi-Dopman & Conway, 2012). For teachers who are overwhelmed with a sizeable workload, however, connecting with parents regularly can be one of the first things that gets overlooked.

Research continually supports the need for effective parent-teacher relationships for the success of the student (Hedeen, Moses, & Marshall, 2011; Magaldi-Dopman & Conway, 2012; Murray, Handyside, Straka, & Arton-Titus, 2013). Why, then, are there barriers to successful communication and how can teachers and parents bridge these barriers to ensure the best outcomes for students?

CHALLENGES TO EFFECTIVE PARENT-TEACHER COMMUNICATION AND COLLABORATION

Since parents and schools are working toward the same goal of student success, it would seem as though parent-teacher communication and collaboration would be a given; however, it is often easier said than done. There are many different beliefs and ideas between teachers and parents that can cause a rift in communication and collaboration efforts (Adams, Harris, & Jones, 2016). Parents can often feel disconnected with the school, which can result in a reluctance to engage with the school until it's too late (Staples & Diliberto, 2010).

Research has shown a strong correlation between parent involvement and student achievement (Magaldi-Dopman & Conway, 2012). Students whose parents actively participate in their education often experience less absences and better overall attitude in school (Sheppard, 2009). This, in turn, positively affects student achievement because the student then feels as though the school is a supportive network. Teachers who regularly collaborate with parents often gain insight into cultural factors that they may not understand otherwise (Lewis, Kim, & Bey, 2011; Magaldi-Dopman & Conway, 2012). When teachers have a solid understanding of their students' home lives, it makes it easier to respond to their students.

Teachers may feel they are not well-equipped to foster effective parent-teacher communication. In some cases, new teachers have not had enough preparation to prepare them for the level of communication they will need to have with parents and caregivers of disabled students (Murray et al., 2013). When there is a breakdown in communication, the lack of home-school continuity negatively impacts the students, resulting in an implicit distrust of the teacher (Magaldi-Dopman & Conway, 2012). This distrust most often occurs when parents feel as though their voices are not being heard or that the school is trying to force them into a decision that they don't understand (Cheatham & Ostrosky, 2011).

Hedeen et al. (2011) explain that there are essentially four stages wherein increased partnership between parents and teachers occurs—informing, involving, engaging, and leading. The first stop on the continuum, informing, is the one-way communication by which the school generally conveys information. The definition of inform means to "communicate knowledge to, to impart information or knowledge" (Merriam-Webster, 2018).

When an individual is told something, there is little room for the individual to provide his or her input. As such, parents who are informed about their child may feel as though they are unable to participate in reciprocal communication (Adams et al., 2016; Hedeen et al., 2011). For parents who are unsure as to how to navigate the educational system, they may feel silenced and invaluable to the child's educational decision-making.

The second stage—involving—asks that parents join in the conversation about the student; however, the involvement the school is looking for is often to support a plan of action that was pre-determined by the school (Hedeen et al., 2011). While parents may feel that involving them in their child's education is a sign that schools want to collaborate, it can often have the opposite effect (Murray et al., 2013). Teachers who have weak communication skills with parents may become overly helpful, providing advice as to what they would do, but not truly appreciating the parents' perspective (Cheatham & Ostrosky, 2011; Patte, 2011).

Engaging is a more inclusive practice, encouraging parents to come together with school staff to create an educational plan or make child-centered decisions (Hedeen et al., 2011). Treating parents as partners in the decision-making process can help to solidify relationships and create trust in the educators with whom their child works. This is especially important during IEP meetings, where parents often feel outside of the team (Feinberg, Moses, Engiles, Whitehorne, & Peter, 2014).

The last stage on the continuum of partnership—leading—occurs when parents have forged a solid foundation of communication and collaboration, resulting in the feeling that they are truly valued team members (Hedeen et al., 2011). This is particularly important for families from socioeconomic, cultural, and educational backgrounds that are different than those of the teacher.

Research suggests that culturally and socioeconomically minority families have difficulties forming solid partnerships with school staff because they feel as though staff are disconnected from their experiences (Cheatham & Ostrosky, 2011; Kroeger & Lash, 2011). This can be especially true for homeless families who are often unsure of how to keep up with their child's educational needs while dealing with an uncertain living situation (National Center for Homeless Education [NCHE], 2015).

A MISUNDERSTANDING OF DISABILITY

As of the 2013–2014 school year, students with disabilities made up approximately 13% of total public-school enrollment (National Center for Education Statistics, 2018). The majority of these students have high-incidence disabilities, which are often categorized as communication disorders, specific learning disorders, and health impairments, such as ADHD (National Center for Education Statistics, 2018). For students with high-incidence disabilities, it is often difficult to distinguish them from general education students as they may not outwardly appear to have any learning challenges, or their learning challenges may manifest as a behavioral concern (Gwernan-Jones et al., 2015).

When disabled students continue to struggle or have behavioral outbursts, studies suggest that teachers often attribute this to poor parenting and lack of interest in the child's educational progress (Broomhead, 2013; Gwernan-Jones et al., 2015). Furthermore, teachers may unintentionally make assumptions about the student's interest and ability in school. This can further segregate parents who may feel as though the school lacks an understanding of the child's disability and, therefore, has little interest in developing a collaborative relationship with the parent of the "problem child."

In a review of the literature on parents' perspectives of ADHD and teacher-parent relationships, Gwernan-Jones et al. (2015) discovered that commonalities existed among parents of students with ADHD in particular, but that could be generalized to other disabilities. This review suggests that parents feel judged by schools based on their child's behaviors in school. Mothers, especially, felt judged harshly by schools based on the assumption that poorly behaved children are lacking in parenting skills (Hibbitts, 2010). Additionally, it was discovered that parents of disabled students report that their child experiences high levels of anxiety when they perceive that their teacher doesn't like them (Carpenter & Austin, 2008).

When parents feel criticized for their parenting skills or lack thereof, whether it's implicitly felt or explicitly stated, they are less likely to want to participate in any type of relationship with the school beyond what is necessary such as parent-teacher conferences, IEP meetings (Murray et al., 2013). Unfortunately, this is further exacerbated by a misunderstanding of the characteristics of a child's disability. Perhaps most importantly, preservice teachers must develop a solid understanding of the ups and down associated with the disabilities of the students they will likely serve (Murray et al., 2013). Both veteran special and general education teachers must go the extra step to ensure that if they don't fully understand the child's disability, they remain open to help from the parent who knows her child best (Margalit, Raskind, Higgins, & Russo-Netzer, 2010).

IN TIMES OF PARENTAL CONFLICT

Creating an effective educational environment for a disabled student takes intense planning and in-depth knowledge of the child's strengths and weaknesses. Oftentimes, the first chance parents and teachers get to hash out the particulars of the child's plan is at the IEP meeting. IEP meetings can be difficult for both families and schools as there can be tension due to disagreements in both the methodology and delivery of services available to the child (Arizona Department of Education, 2018).

In the case of two-parent households, most of the time these parents form an allied front against the school when they believe their child deserves more than what the school is proposing. During these times, schools can remind parents of the dispute resolution process available under IDEA (2004) in which they can pursue assistance in settling their argument with the school or filing a formal complaint; however, although rare, there are instances when both parents conflict with each other, creating a different type of tension among IEP team members.

Parents of children with disabilities face stressors that other parents may not as they may have to juggle medical and related service appointments, financial strain related to the child's disability and time needed off from work, and social isolation as a result of the time required to be spent on the child's needs, which increases the rate of depression for these parents (Feinberg et al., 2014).

Parents of disabled children often lack the familial and community supports needed to help manage the stress related to the demands of raising a child with special needs. It can be especially stressful on the family unit when the child has a severe disability that requires an intense level of care (Tint & Weiss, 2016; Walton, 2016). In addition to dealing with the stress of the disability, parents are often dealing with the grief associated with having a child who will struggle his or her whole life (Boushey, 2001).

It should come as no surprise, then, that yearly IEP meetings would be stressful for parents, especially for parents who cannot agree on the most appropriate services and supports for their child. School staff are generally prepared for contentious meetings between the school and the family; however, staff are not often prepared to handle meetings that quickly devolve into conflict between parents. Staff may be afraid to attempt to mediate the conflict because they do not want to appear to take sides. Feinberg et al. (2014) suggest several ways that the school can mitigate the impact of inter-parental conflict before the meeting takes place.

- Schools should self-assess to ensure that they have procedures in place to handle and manage conflict during meetings. This could include having a third-party facilitator present or building the capacity of current staff to help objectively resolve the conflict.
- Ongoing professional development should be provided to staff who participate in IEP meetings so that they can become familiar with possible scenarios that may occur during these meetings. Training staff on cultural sensitivity practices can also be helpful in understanding parental conflict and helping to lessen its impact on the team.
- Use team planning time to discuss potentially tense situations before the team meeting occurs. Speaking to other team members about concerns and developing a plan of action for handling conflict can lessen the stress on team members and help them to go into the meeting more clear-headed.
- Electronic communication can be helpful, especially in instances where parents cannot be in the same room with each other. Options such as Skype allow parents to participate without physically being in the room. However, teams must keep in mind that arguments can still occur, so conflict resolution skills are continually needed.
- Use of parent mentors can be effective when all other options have been exhausted. Parent mentors support both the parent and educators with information at team meetings. These support personnel often work with

divorced or separating parents to ensure that the educational needs of the child are still met regardless of the conflict between the parents.

Feinberg et al. (2014) also suggest steps that can be taken during the meeting to provide for the comfort of all participants. Scheduling meeting times that are convenient for the family and fellow staff members can ensure that all participants have sufficient time to share information about the student, ensuring that seating arrangements are conducive to collaborative discussion is crucial, especially with parents who are either in conflict with the school or with each other are two important considerations (Feinberg et al., 2014). Providing meeting participants with an agenda can also help to keep meetings on track and reminding participants of the time limit can prevent discussions from going off track (Feinberg et al., 2014).

It is crucial to remember that the focus of the meeting is the child, and it can be difficult to maintain that focus when parents are arguing with each other during the meeting; however, schools must remember that they are in charge of the meeting and they can choose to adjourn the meeting if the level of tension impacts productivity. In most cases, both parents want what is best for their child and it is the role of the school to help them come to an agreement that is beneficial for the student.

WHEN SCHOOLS FAIL TO PLAN APPROPRIATELY FOR POST-SECONDARY NEEDS

One of the major points of contention between parents and schools is the perceived lack of concern in planning for the student. This is especially true for older children with disabilities who require transition planning services. For a student to experience successful post-secondary outcomes, it is necessary to have the support of both the family and the school (Lindstrom et al., 2007).

Parents are often unaware about transition planning and the processes by which their child can receive post-secondary support (Miller-Warren, 2016). Parents rely on the school to help with this process, yet many schools fail to provide what parents view as appropriate supports. Transition planning often occurs during the annual IEP review meeting, and oftentimes little attention is paid to the careful development of a meaningful plan of action. Parents have reported feeling confused and frustrated with the school's lack of interest in both their input and their child's interests (Miller-Warren, 2016).

Schools are responsible for developing a plan of action based on the child's desires for what he or she would like to do after high school, whether that be college or the workforce. Once the school puts this plan into place, collaboration must occur between the school, the parent, and the outside agencies through which services are obtained to ensure the student experiences a smooth transition from high school to adulthood (Ankeny, Wilkins, & Spain, 2009; Miller-Warren, 2016). Many parents report that schools lack the sense of urgency to start the transition process, and they often feel that schools try to pigeonhole their child into a career in which he or she is not interested (Curtis, Rabren, & Reilly, 2009).

Schools must remember that planning for a disabled child does not solely occur within the confines of the six-hour school day. Students with disabilities have a range of needs that must be addressed to help them become successful, contributing citizens. Parents who feel dismissed by staff when planning for the student's post-secondary life are likely to distrust the decisions made by staff during the school day (Adams et al., 2016; Miller-Warren, 2016). Encouraging a sense of trust in the parent is the foundation for creating a solid collaborative partnership.

BRIDGING THE GAP BETWEEN MISTRUST AND COLLABORATION

It may seem overwhelming for teachers to prepare for the multitude of possible interactions with parents. Knowing that some discussions will be difficult can help teachers better prepare themselves to handle conflict. The following are some additional suggestions for creating a mutually respectful relationship with parents in which they are happy to participate.

- **Appreciate cultural differences.** Understanding that each culture has its own set of expectations that may not fall in line with the teacher's background can help with creating an effective plan for the student (Gwernan-Jones et al., 2015). For instance, being cognizant of the ways in which gender roles are perceived by different cultures is important when conducting an IEP meeting. Families who defer to the father's choices may have difficulty responding when staff address the mother during the meeting (Feinberg et al., 2014).
- **Listen to parents.** It is easy to become dismissive of parents' concerns, especially when the school sees one type of behavior but the parent reports something entirely different; however, parents want to be heard and have their concerns taken seriously (Murray et al., 2013). Because school staff are often seen as the experts when it comes to knowledge about a disability, it is easy for parents to defer to staff's recommendations without challenging them (Broomhead, 2013; Gwernan-Jones et al., 2015). Taking the time to sit down with parents and really hear their concerns will go a long way in encouraging a sense of trust in the parent. Regardless of the ultimate team decision, at least the parents will feel as though their con-

cerns were heard and considered, and that they helped to shape their child's education plan.
- **Extend help and knowledge.** Parents often come to the process of special education without any idea about the complex processes that await them. It is the job of the educators to extend their knowledge to the parent, so the process becomes a little less daunting. It is easy for school staff to become defensive when parents' perceptions do not align with their own; however, oftentimes parents' lack of knowledge is a barrier to clear communication (Murray et al., 2013).

  A parent, for example, may feel that because their child is not reading at grade level, he or she must have a specific learning disability; however, as school staff know, there are a multitude of factors that can impact a student's ability to read at grade level. Without educating the parent on possible interventions that can help the child before special education services even begin, the school may inadvertently create a tense relationship where the parent feels dismissed, and the child fails to receive intervention in a timely manner.
- **Include, include, include.** It may seem daunting to consider contacting parents every day or calling them to alert them to a seemingly small change in the classroom; however, these communications are appreciated by parents more than educators may realize (Adams et al., 2016; Cheatham & Ostrosky, 2010; Magaldi-Dopman & Conway, 2012). If the goal is to create a truly collaborative relationship with the parent, the school must be willing to extend themselves in such a way that shows the parent they are a valued member of the child's team. Many parents are only contacted a few times a year, mostly for bi-annual parent-teacher conferences and annual IEP meetings (Murray et al., 2013). Reaching out proactively will convey the message that the parent is an integral partner in their child's educational planning.

FINAL THOUGHTS

Parents clearly want to collaborate with schools, but they often experience barriers to successfully doing so. Teachers and school staff must be cognizant of the challenges parents face when trying to navigate the complex process of special education. Reaching out to parents and providing them assistance with understanding their role in the educational planning of their child can go a long way in forging a collaborative partnership with a parent. Additionally, creating an environment in which the parents' perspectives are both expected and welcome is crucial in creating a comprehensive educational plan for a student.

While there are many challenges that can hinder the parent-teacher relationship, the end goal is to work together to provide the most appropriate educational experience for the student. Appreciating cultural and socioeconomic differences and working to understand the stressors within the home can help teachers to gain a clearer picture of the impact these can have on working with the student. Being willing to work with the family in the pursuit of positive educational outcomes is one of many steps necessary for helping a disabled student achieve success; however, going the extra mile to communicate and collaborate regularly can exponentially increase student success.

POINTS TO REMEMBER

- Research continually supports the need for effective parent-teacher relationships for the success of the student.
- Teachers who regularly collaborate with parents often gain insight into cultural factors that they may not understand otherwise.
- Some obstacles to effective parent-teacher communication and collaboration include a misunderstanding of the student's disability on the part of the staff, understanding how to work effectively with parents who are in conflict with each other, and not identifying the appropriate supports for students with disabilities.
- Ways to improve parent-teacher communication and collaboration include appreciating cultural differences, extend help and knowledge when applicable, listen intently to parents' concerns and include these concerns in the educational planning process, and include parents in all aspects of the child's educational experience.

Chapter Ten

Transition Planning

Ensuring Successful Post-Secondary Outcomes for Students with Disabilities

Transition planning and assessments are two of the most critical, yet often overlooked, components of the IEP. It is the school's responsibility to be sure that disabled students have access to post-secondary opportunities and supports that will help them make a smooth transition into adulthood (Rehfeldt, Clark, & Lee, 2012). Unfortunately, many schools don't allot enough time for transition planning and assessment, nor do they consistently involve parents and students, which creates a disadvantage (Campbell, Baxter, Ellis, & Pardue, 2013; Miller-Warren, 2016).

For students with disabilities, gaining meaningful employment without assistance is difficult at best. Stevenson and Fowler (2016) cite data indicating that only 60% of out-of-school individuals with disabilities had found employment. Of that percentage, only 52% earned the minimum wage, and 40.2% worked more than 35 hours per week (Stevenson & Fowler, 2016). These statistics are alarming as they suggest a lack of employable skills within the population of disabled youth.

It is the school's obligation to help provide planning that will allow these students to develop job-related skills, as well as to put these students in contact with job-shadowing and internship opportunities (Stevenson & Fowler, 2016). This will provide the foundation needed to help them gain employment in a field of their choosing (Stevenson & Fowler, 2016). Oftentimes, school staff are misinformed about the need for in-depth transition planning, which comes at a cost to the student; therefore, it is necessary for special educators to understand the often-misunderstood process.

WHAT IS TRANSITION PLANNING AND WHY IS IT NEEDED?

Transition planning and assessment are mandated under IDEA (2004). Students are required to be assessed for their career interests, and from there team members work to develop a plan of action complete with goals that guide the student in the direction of his or her career choice (Trainor, Morningstar, & Murray, 2016). The most successful transition planning is outcome-oriented and provides a specific sequence of steps that help the student reach his or her post-secondary goals (Statfeld, 2011).

Typically, transition planning must take place by the time the student reaches the age of 16, although some states require it take place as young as 14 years of age (IDEA, 2004; Statfeld, 2011; Trainor et al., 2016). Transition planning at this age is important, as that is often when adolescents become eligible for employment in their respective state. Beginning to focus the student toward his or her interests at this age can help them make informed decisions about future career aspirations (Collier, Griffin, & Wei, 2016).

Aside from the fact that transition planning and assessment are required by law, special educators have an obligation to their students to help them overcome the obstacles that pose challenges not faced by the general population. For disabled students, aspiring to a career often feels overwhelming; for example, students with physical disabilities may not have the same opportunities as others because they may have reduced range of motion. This would preclude them from choosing certain careers (Osgood, Foster, & Courtney, 2010). Without support, these students may not find options within their chosen field that are suitable to their physical limitations.

Some disabled students have deficiencies in family support (Osgood et al., 2010). These deficiencies range from parents who are unsure how to access post-secondary services to parents who are altogether absent (Osgood et al., 2010). There are service agencies through which students can gain support; however, the process through which students must go is complex and difficult to navigate without the assistance of a teacher or counselor (Statfeld, 2011). For students who have mild disabilities or who plan to attend college, assistance is still needed to help guide them through the college and workforce application process. Oftentimes students with milder disabilities are excluded from the supports available to all students with disabilities because they appear to be able to navigate the requirements on their own; however, educators should not assume that support is not needed.

TRANSITION ASSESSMENTS: WHAT ARE THEY AND HOW DO THEY WORK?

There is no one-size-fits-all approach to transition assessments. There are many different tools used to help the student decide which career options are a good fit. Perhaps the most well-known assessment, the Transition Planning Inventory (TPI), was created to develop a helpful framework from which schools could structure transition planning activities (Clark & Patton, 2006). The TPI is based on the simple premise that assessment from home, school, and the student can lead to the creation of goals and objectives which will then lead to the development of actionable steps that the student can take to move toward his or her career outcome (Rehfeldt et al., 2012).

The TPI provides an evaluation of the student in nine domains to include employment, further education/training, daily living, leisure activities, community participation, health, self-determination, communication, and interpersonal relationships (Clark & Patton, 2006; Rehfeldt et al., 2012). Each of these domains is important to the success of the student once he or she leaves his or her educational setting. The assessment has forms for the parents, student, and school personnel, which should all be completed to get the most comprehensive understanding of what the child can do and where he or she may need more assistance (Clark & Patton, 2006). The forms are scored, and answers are given values based on averages from all three raters (Clark & Patton, 2006). These scores give the examiner an understanding of which careers may be fitting for the student.

Another tool used by teams to help with transition services is the summary of performance (SOP). IDEA (2004) requires that schools complete a summary of student performance as part of the exit requirements for students with disabilities (Shaw, Dukes, & Madaus, 2012). This document summarizes both academic achievement and functional performance, as well as includes recommendations from the school on how to help the student meet his or her preferred post-secondary goals.

There are five components to the SOP to include background information, post-secondary goals, summary of performance, recommendations, and student input (Shaw et al., 2012). Unfortunately, there is no set substantive criteria that must be included in the SOP. Districts are at their own discretion when filling out this document, and like transition planning, the SOP often becomes an afterthought at team meetings. Shaw et al. (2012) provide some suggestions on how to best incorporate the SOP into transition planning so that it is a valuable exercise and document.

- Begin the SOP early enough so that it can be reviewed over time with the student. Do not wait until the student is graduating to complete the document. Reviewing the SOP with the student can be helpful in monitoring

his or her progress toward goals and can help the team determine which transition needs must be addressed.
- Develop a portfolio that has a method of tracking data over time. It will then be easier to incorporate necessary data into the SOP, allowing for easier assessment of progress on goals.
- Have the student lead the discussion of his or her own performance whenever possible. This can help promote the types of post-secondary skills the student will need and will allow the team to directly hear from the student about his or her aspirations and what he or she feels needs more work.
- Involve as many stakeholders as possible. Do not merely rely on the special education teacher and parent to provide the most input. Teams should consist of various staff members with whom the student has worked over the course of his or her time in high school. Relying on a small sampling of people is detrimental to planning a well-rounded plan of action for the student.

There are also some transition assessment tools that have been piloted to determine their effectiveness at helping students, parents, and schools with transition planning. The CHOICES Project, funded by the Institute of Education Sciences, provides parents, schools, students, and community agencies with access to information regarding transitional support programs (Campbell et al., 2013). The project consists of two databases, one that includes student information and another that includes community information, as well as several transition-type applications (surveys, questionnaires, etc.), and a website with transition-related content (Campbell et al., 2013). The goal of this project is to provide positive transition outcomes for students and families who feel disconnected from the school-based transition planning process. Campbell et al. (2013) reported positive functionality of the program, although more funding is required to continue with research.

Another study performed by Collier and colleagues (2016) examined the effectiveness of the Student Transition Questionnaire (STQ), which was designed to provide teachers with a tool that was both easy-to-use and socially valid, focusing on gathering students' perspectives on a wide range of transition issues. The STQ consists of 200 items that were created from a review of the literature on transition planning and assessments (Collier et al., 2016).

The items, while similar to the items on the TPI, are more in-depth, yet simpler to understand. Some examples of the items on the STQ include, "I can follow doctor's orders and take prescriptions correctly," "I can plan and save money for big purchases, taxes, etc.," and "I can name community resources that can help me" (Collier et al., 2016, p. 5). Although this pilot study employed a small sampling of subjects, the researchers conclude that the STQ shows promise in including student perspectives into the transition-planning process (Collier et al., 2016). Students with learning disabilities were successful in completing the STQ, which shows promise for the future of the assessment.

TRANSITION ACTIVITIES: WHEN ARE THEY PERFORMED AND WHO IS RESPONSIBLE?

When thinking about formulating a comprehensive transition plan for a student, it's clear that one of the key components is to begin early and continue adding relevant information to it as the student gets older. It is also important to ensure that all team members understand their role in the planning process. Roles are interchangeable; while some schools have transition planning specialists, others utilize teachers to do most of the legwork for the planning phase (Stevenson & Fowler, 2016). Team members must remember that they are all responsible for being a part of the transition process and should contribute as much as they can to increase the chances of a positive postsecondary outcome for the student.

The following are some transition activities to consider, and the times at which to consider them, when preparing a student for his or her post-secondary goals. This is not an exhaustive list and should be used to supplement the transition requirements provided by each respective school district (adapted from the Statfeld, 2011).

Four to Five Years Before the Student Leaves the District

- Identify the student's learning styles and the most appropriate accommodations that the child will need to be successful.
- Identify the student's career interests and skills, complete transition assessments, such as the TPI, and identify further areas of training or education needed.
- Identify the post-secondary admissions criteria for the colleges of the student's choice.
- Determine the student's choice for living arrangements after high school.
- Educate the student on the ways in which to explain his or her disability and to ask for assistance and accommodations.
- Teach the student about health care, money management, and securing community resources.

Two to Three Years Before the Student Leaves the District

- Identify and contact community support services, such as vocational rehabilitation or Department of Developmental Services.

- Help the student to match his or her career interests to work and community experiences.
- Help the student obtain more in-depth information about colleges and the support services they offer.
- Help students understand the college admissions process, as well as how to obtain financial aid.
- Work with the student to develop improved interpersonal skills for such situations as job interviews and employee/customer interactions.
- Begin the discussion around age of majority and the legal requirements surrounding the decision-making process.

One Year Before Leaving the School District

- Help the student apply for financial support programs, where applicable.
- Help the student to navigate public transportation services, if needed.
- Further help the student to improve his or her communication skills.
- Assist the student with understanding his or her new role as an adult. Providing help with things such as understanding health insurance coverage, registering to vote, and making doctor's appointments is crucial in preparing the student to function independently.
- Provide support to the student as he or she seeks out paid employment, and coach the student on the ways in which to meet attendance and conduct policies.

It is more important to ensure that these and similar activities are completed with the student than it is to have hard and fast rules about who is responsible for each activity. There has been extensive research cited in the literature suggesting that transition planning is a major area in which schools fall short; therefore, it is crucial for schools to focus on rectifying this problem (Ankeny et al., 2009; Campbell et al., 2013; Collier et al., 2016; Miller-Warren, 2016; Osgood et al., 2010; Trainor et al., 2016).

FINAL THOUGHTS

Ensuring the smooth transition from high school to post-secondary life is necessary for students with disabilities. Not only is transition planning and assessment required under IDEA (2004), but it also in the best interest of the student to have assistance with understanding how to navigate the complexities of adulthood. As more students qualify for special education services, the need for effective transition planning is crucial to providing well-rounded comprehensive services for students with disabilities.

Parents report that schools have historically been dismissive of the post-secondary needs of disabled students, and this must be rectified. Parents who have reported that the school's transition planning process had a negative impact on their child's post-secondary success are more likely to have children who are unemployed and still live at home (Miller-Warren, 2016). Conversely, research shows that students can gain more positive outcomes after high school when they experience a solid transition planning process (Oertle & Trach, 2007).

A successful process consists of continued collaboration among parents, students, school, and community agencies. While the school's direct role may end when the student is no longer enrolled in the district, if it has done a successful job in readying the student for transition, its influence can be felt through the connections made with post-secondary systems of support.

POINTS TO REMEMBER

- It is the school's responsibility to be sure that disabled students have access to post-secondary opportunities and supports that will help them make a smooth transition into adulthood.
- The most successful transition planning is outcome-oriented and provides a specific sequence of steps that help the student reach his or her post-secondary goals.
- Transition planning must take place by the time the student reaches the age of 16, although some states require it take place as young as 14 years of age.
- There is no one-size-fits-all approach to transition assessments. There are many different tools and assessments that can help schools, parents, and students to discover career options that are the best fit for the student.
- Team members must remember that they are all responsible for being a part of the transition process and should contribute as much as they can to increase the chances of a positive post-secondary outcome for the student.
- When thinking about formulating a comprehensive transition plan for a student, it's clear that one of the key components is to begin early and continue adding relevant information to it as the student gets older.

Chapter Eleven

Resources to Support Special Education Professionals

Working in special education can be challenging, especially for new teachers. Oftentimes, teachers may feel as though they don't have enough strategies in their toolbox to address all the concerns they may face. Conversely, teachers who have been in the field for several years may find that they need new strategies to supplement methods that are already successful. Luckily, in today's world, resources are always available at one's fingertips. The following section offers a suggestive list of some supports for special education teachers, ranging from activities and curriculum planning to legal assistance. While this is not an exhaustive list by any means, it may provide new and seasoned educators with additional tools to help increase their repertoire of strategies.

ACTIVITIES AND GAMES

- **Do2Learn:** This site provides thousands of free pages of strategies and interventions to help with social skills development, behavior regulation, communication, and even transition and employment skills. Do2Learn was born in 1996 from a National Institutes of Health grant, in which teachers and clinicians from all over the world lent their knowledge, creativity, and expertise to help create resources for other special educators. In addition to providing interaction and printable material for special education teachers, the site also provides visitors with information about disabilities, the evaluation process, and strategies to help parents and teachers successfully collaborate. For more information, visit www.do2learn.com

- **Education World:** Education World is a comprehensive online resource for teachers, administrators, and school staff providing high-quality content that is updated daily. This site has been active since 1996, and it provides educators with news and learning activities that can be used within the classroom. Subject areas addressed on the site include all core subjects (English, math, science, and social studies), as well as physical education, arts, and humanities. The site even has an area for gifted and talented students who may need a bit of an extra challenge. In addition to the interactive games and activities for students, the site offers lesson plans and professional development opportunities for staff. For more information, visit https://www.educationworld.com
- **IXL Worldwide:** IXL offers technology-based, interactive learning for students with disabilities. Aligned with the Common Core Standards, IXL offers content from pre–K through 12th grade in all core subject areas. Students can utilize the platform both at school and at home. The site even offers motivational "rewards" such as virtual stickers at the end of each mastered lesson. IXL content changes as the student masters a concept, so the activities are based on what the child can do at any given time. IXL activities can provide diagnostic information to teachers that then allows them to tailor lessons to address the student's areas of deficit. For more information, visit https://www.ixl.com
- **FunBrain:** Created in 1997, FunBrain offers arcade-style learning games for students with disabilities in grades K–8. The site offers tutorial videos and practice games that grab the student's attention with titles like "Math Baseball" and "When Pigs Fly." In addition to games, FunBrain offers books, comics, and videos that can help students develop skills in math, reading, problem-solving, and literacy. For more information, visit https://www.funbrain.com
- **Learning Ally:** This national nonprofit, which has been in business for 70 years, provides disabled students with access to audiobooks. Students with disabilities ranging from visual impairments to dyslexia benefit from Learning Ally's technology. Their mission is to ensure that all students have the equal opportunity to learn irrespective of disability. What makes this organization unique is that volunteers who have in-depth knowledge of subject matter are trained to read and describe the content in each of the books available on the site; for example, readers describe visuals such as pictures and charts, as well as mathematical equations. Learning Ally partners with all major textbook publishing companies; thus, it is likely students will be able to find their textbook among the 80,000 titles offered. For more information, visit https://www.learningally.org

CURRICULUM AND PLANNING

- **TeacherVision:** TeacherVision is a site that includes resources ranging from curriculum strategies and classroom management supports, to working with students with specific disabilities. Included on the website are printables such as behavior charts, accommodations checklists, and planning worksheets, as well as resources for working with students who have autism spectrum disorder and ADHD. In addition to disability resources, the site also includes resources for working with English language learners. TeacherVision offers suggestions for teachers who work with assistive technology and provides resources for students who need educational technology as part of their program. For more information, visit https://www.teachervision.com
- **Newsela:** Newsela is a digital platform for reading that provides differentiated, high-interest texts aligned to curricula and updated daily. What makes Newsela unique is that a full classroom of students can read the same text, however the program levels it for the individual student; therefore, two seventh-grade students, one reading at a fifth-grade level and one reading at grade level, can access the same text and participate in the same lesson without the teacher needing to slow the class pace or group students based on reading level. In addition to providing reading support, Newsela also has social-emotional learning content weaved into its programming. For more information, visit https://newsela.com
- **Lesson Planet:** Lesson Planet is an online search engine of over 350,000 teacher-reviewed curriculum resources. Founded in 1999, Lesson Planet's team of licensed teachers reviews lesson plan submissions and resources to ensure quality and alignment with Common Core Standards. Lesson Planet has won several awards, which attests to its value for teachers across the country. This is a paid-membership site, but memberships range from individual teacher to full districts. For more information, visit https://www.lessonplanet.com
- **Learning Disabilities Online:** LD Online is a site that compiles both disability information and teaching resources to help educators working with students with learning disabilities and ADHD. Visitors can discover articles, multimedia, and resource guides with directories to other professionals. LD Online is a type of "one stop shop" for information and lesson planning resources. The website includes links to other national organizations, as well as to other sites that offer helpful information about learning disabilities. For more information, visit www.ldonline.org

Chapter 11

NEWS AND INFORMATION

- **National Association of Special Education Teachers (NASET):** NASET is the only national membership association with the sole aim of meeting the needs of both new and veteran special education teachers. NASET helps members stay informed of the most current issues impacting the field of special education, including factors influencing the careers of special educators. The organization encourages professional development and continued scholarship in the field, and it purports to help support high-quality special education programs nationwide. Membership to NASET can either be purchased in one- or two-year increments, and it includes free professional development courses, weekly newsletters, and lists of special education forms, tables, checklists, and procedures. For more information, visit https://www.naset.org
- **National Education Association (NEA):** While the NEA is not specifically a special education resource, it does provide the most up-to-date information on public education in the United States. Founded in 1857, the NEA has been advancing the cause for the rights of both students and educators. The NEA publishes a journal four times each year covering the most up-to-date teaching challenges, best practices in education, and most relevant resources for both veteran and new teachers. Additionally, the NEA publishes an annual journal for future teachers that helps readers with job searches, classroom tips and strategies, and resources for working collaboratively with parents. For more information, visit www.nea.org
- **National Center for Learning Disabilities (NCLD):** The mission statement of the NCLD purports to "improve the lives of the one in five children and adults nationwide with learning and attention issues" through helping parents and young adults to advocate for equal rights and opportunities for the learning disabled. Founded in 1977, the NCLD provides leadership, public awareness of disabilities, and grants for further research and program development. The NCLD website provides resources for understanding self-advocacy, legalities surrounding disability law, and access to further information about programming for parents, young adults, professionals, and educators. For more information, visit https://www.ncld.org
- **Social Media:** Not surprisingly, sites such as Facebook, Twitter, and LinkedIn can provide special educators with access to additional resources. On Facebook, educators can search for special education teacher groups that can be joined in order to connect with other like-minded individuals in the same teaching field. Twitter includes experts and teachers who tweet news, information, and updated resources, which may be helpful for teachers who are looking to stay on top of the latest developments in special education. LinkedIn is a social networking site for professionals,

and educators can create profiles that will then link them in with others within their local professional network. For more information, visit https://www.opencolleges.edu.au/informed/features/social-media-tools-for-education/

LAWS

- **The Education Commission of the States (ESC):** The ESC provides news, research, and special education laws by state. The website also lists special education workshops by area that focus on the needs of special education students. Networking with others within the local area or across the nation is also a possibility through the ESC website. The purpose of the site is to partner with education policy leaders to address education issues through the sharing of resources and expertise. For more information, visit https://www.ecs.org
- **Individuals with Disabilities Education Act (IDEA):** The IDEA's website provides visitors with an in-depth look at the specifics of the IDEA in each of its iterations, as well as links to other government resources on education, such as the Office of Special Education and Rehabilitative Services and the US Department of Education. Also available on the IDEA website is a list of reports that visitors can view highlighting state performance, state monitoring data, and annual planning information. Additionally, IDEA provides visitors with up-to-date news on recent changes to special education law, as well as newsletters and social media sites that address similar issues. For more information, visit https://sites.ed.gov/idea
- **Office of Special Education and Rehabilitative Services (OSERS):** OSERS is comprised of both the Office of Special Education Programs (OSEP) and the Rehabilitation Services Administration (RSA). Both components are committed to improving outcomes for people with disabilities of all ages. OSERS is concerned with ensuring that individuals from pre-K through adulthood have access to quality services and programs that support their development. OSERS is also committed to reducing discrimination among individuals with disabilities and providing education to the public on the laws surrounding disabled individuals. For more information, visit https://www2.ed.gov/about/offices/list/osers/index.html
- **Individual State Websites:** Each state has its own educational governing board. In Massachusetts, for example, there is the Department of Elementary and Secondary Education, or DESE (http://www.doe.mass.edu/). When visiting the DESE website, one can find information about state general and special education laws, assessment data, and school performance. Other states have similar sites that are relevant to both the public and educators. When working in special education it is crucial to become

familiar with the state's website to ensure a complete understanding of the ways in which state laws often differ from federal law. State laws that are more stringent than federal laws are the laws to which special educators must comply. In order to avoid a sticky legal situation, it is necessary to understand all laws that pertain to special education.

References

Adams, D., Harris, A., & Jones, M. S. (2016). Teacher-parent collaboration for an inclusive classroom: Success for every child. *Malaysian Online Journal of Educational Sciences, 4*(3), 58–72. Retrieved from https://files.eric.ed.gov/fulltext/EJ1106456.pdf

ADA National Network. (2015). *An overview of the Americans with Disabilities Act*. Retrieved from https://www.adapacific.org/assets/documents/ada-overview.pdf

Al Otaiba, S. Connor, C. M., Folsom, J. S., Wanzek, J., Greulich, L., Schatschneider, C., & Wagner, R. K. (2014). To wait in tier 1 or intervene immediately: A randomized experiment examining first grade response to intervention (RTI) in reading. *Exceptional Children, 81*(1) 11–27. Retrieved from https://eric.ed.gov/?id=ED562485

American Printing House for the Blind. (2016). *Annual report 2016: Distribution of eligible students based on federal quota census of January 3, 2015 (fiscal year 2016)*. Retrieved from http://aph.org/federal-quota/distribution-of-students-2016/

American Psychiatric Association. (2017). *What is intellectual disability?* Retrieved from https://www.psychiatry.org/patients-families/intellectual-disability/what-is-intellectual-disability.

American Speech-Language-Hearing Association [ASHA]. (n.d.). *Types of hearing loss*. Retrieved from https://www.asha.org/public/hearing/types-of-hearing-loss/

American Speech-Language-Hearing Association [ASHA]. (1999). *Learning disabilities: Use of paraprofessionals*. Retrieved from https://www.asha.org/policy/RP1999-00128.htm

American Speech-Language-Hearing Association [ASHA]. (2010). *Roles and responsibilities of speech-language pathologists in schools*. Retrieved from https://www.asha.org/policy/PI2010-00317/

Ankeny, E., Wilkins, J., & Spain, J. (2009). Mothers' experiences of transition planning for their children with disabilities. *Teaching Exceptional Children, 41*(6), 28–36. DOI: 10.1177/004005990904100604

Ansley, B. M., Houchins, D., & Varjas, K. (2016). Optimizing special educator wellness and job performance through stress management. *Teaching Exceptional Children, 48*(4), 176–185. DOI: 10.1177/00400599156128

Arizona Department of Education. (2018). *Consensus*. Retrieved from http://www.azed.gov/disputeresolution/category/consensus/

Bambrick-Santoyo, P. (2010). *Driven by data: A practical guide to improve instruction*. San Francisco, CA: Jossey-Bass.

Barnes, C. S., Dunning, J. L., & Rehfeldt, R. A. (2011). An evaluation of strategies for training staff to implement the picture exchange communication system. *Research in Autism Spectrum Disorders, 5*(4), 1574–1583. DOI: 10.1016/j.rasd.2011.03.003

References

Bateman, D., & Bateman, J. (2014). *A principal's guide to special education.* Arlington, VA: Council for Exceptional Children.

Bateman, D., & Cline, J. (2016). *A teachers guide to special education.* Alexandria, VA: ASCD.

Bateman, D., & Herr, C. (2010). *Writing measurable IEP goals and objectives.* Verona, WI: Attainment Company.

Binet, A., & Simon, T. (1916). *The development of intelligence in children.* Baltimore, MD: Williams & Wilkins.

Blerklom, M. (2017). *Measurement and statistics for teachers.* New York, NY: Routledge.

Boushey, A. (2001). The grief cycle: One parent's trip around. *Focus on Autism and Other Developmental Disabilities, 16*(1), 27–30. DOI: 10.1177/108835760101600107

Boyle, C., & Topping, K. (2012). *What works in inclusion?* New York, NY: Open University Press.

Braaten, E. (2018). *The SAGE encyclopedia of intellectual and developmental disorders.* Thousand Oaks, CA: Sage.

Bradshaw, C., Koth, C., Thorton, L, & Leaf, P. (2009). Altering school climate through school wide positive behavioral interventions and supports: Findings from a group randomized effectiveness trial. *Prevention Science, 10*(2), 100–115. DOI: 10.1007/s11121-008-0114-9

Bradshaw, C., Waasdorp, T., & Leaf, P. (2012). Effects of school wide positive behavioral interventions and supports on child behavior problems. *American Academy of Pediatrics, 130*(5), e1136–e1145. Retrieved from http://pediatrics.aappublications.org/content/130/5/e1136

Breton, W. (2010). Special education paraprofessionals: Perceptions of preservice preparation, supervision, and ongoing developmental training. *International Journal of Special Education, 25*(1), 34–45. Retrieved from https://eric.ed.gov/?id=EJ890564

Brock, M. E., & Carter, E. W. (2015a). Efficacy of teachers training paraprofessionals to implement peer support arrangements. *Exceptional Children, 82*(3), 354–371. DOI: 10.1177/0014402915585564

Brock, M. E. & Carter, E. W. (2015b). Effects of a professional development package to prepare special education paraprofessionals to implement evidence-based practices. *The Journal of Special Education, 49*(1), 39–51. DOI: 10.1177/0022466913501882

Brookman-Frazee, L. I., Taylor, R., & Garland, A. F. (2010). Characterizing community-based mental health services for children with autism spectrum disorders and disruptive behavior problems. *Journal of Autism and Developmental Disorders, 40*(10), 1188–1201. DOI: 10.1007/s10803-010-0976-0

Broomhead, K. (2013). Blame, guilt and the need for "labels": Insights from parents' children with special educational needs and educational practitioners. *British Journal of Special Education, 40*(1), 14–21. DOI: 10.1111/1467-8578.12012

Brown-Chidsey, R., & Bickford, R. (2016). *Practical handbook of multi-tiered systems of support.* New York, NY: Guilford Press.

Brown, R., & Steege, M. (2011). *Response to intervention: Principles and strategies for effective practice.* New York, NY: Guilford Press.

Bryant, D., Smith, B., & Bryant, B. (2016). *Teaching students with special needs in inclusive classrooms.* London, UK: Pearson.

Buffum, A., Mattos, M., & Weber, C. (2012). *Simplifying response to intervention: Four essential guiding principles.* Bloomington, IN: Solution Tree Press.

Burke, M. M., & Goldman, S. E. (2017). Documenting the experiences of special education advocates. *The Journal of Special Education, 51*(1), 3–13. DOI: 10.1177/0022466916643714

Burns, E. (2007). *The essential special education guide for the regular education teacher.* Springfield, IL: Charles C. Thomas Publisher.

Burns, M. K., & Gibbons, K. (2017). *Implementing response-to-intervention in elementary and secondary schools: Procedures to assure scientific-based practices.* New York, NY: Routledge.

Burton, N. (2018). *Creating effective IEPs: A guide to developing, writing, and implementing plans for teachers.* Thousand Oaks, CA: Sage.

Campbell, D., Baxter, A., Ellis, D., & Pardue, H. (2013). The CHOICES project: Piloting a secondary transition planning database. Paper presented at the Society for Information Technology & Teacher Education (SITE) International Conference. Retrieved from https://files.eric.ed.gov/fulltext/ED543389.pdf

Carpenter, L., & Austin, H. (2008). How to be recognized enough to be included. *International Journal of Inclusive Education, 12*, 35–48. DOI: 10.1080/13603110701683170

Carr, J., & Bertrando, S. (2012). Top 10 instructional strategies for struggling students. *Leadership, 42*(1), 24–26. Retrieved from https://files.eric.ed.gov/fulltext/EJ983557.pdf

CAST. (2018). *UDL at a glance*. Retrieved from http://www.cast.org/our-work/about-udl.html#.W9poaZNKg2w

Catts, H., Nielsen, D., Bridges, M, Lui, Y., & Bontempo, D. (2015). Early identification of reading disabilities within an RTI framework. *Journal of Learning Disabilities, 48*(3), 281–297. DOI: 10.1177/0022219413498115

Celli, L., & Young, N. D. (2014). *Learnings styles perspectives: The impact in the classroom* (3rd ed.). Madison, WI: Atwood Publishing.

Center for Parent Information & Resources. (2015a). *Deaf-blindness*. Retrieved from https://www.parentcenterhub.org/deafblindness/

Center for Parent Information & Resources. (2015b). *Multiple disabilities*. Retrieved from https://www.parentcenterhub.org/multiple/

Center for Parent Information & Resources. (2015c). *Deafness and hearing loss*. Retrieved from https://www.parentcenterhub.org/hearingloss/#about

Center for Parent Information & Resources. (2017a). *Special Education*. Retrieved from https://www.parentcenterhub.org/iep-specialeducation/#definition

Center for Parent Information & Resources. (2017b). *Visual impairment, including blindness*. Retrieved from https://www.parentcenterhub.org/visualimpairment/

Center for Parent Information & Resources. (2017c). *Emotional disturbance*. Retrieved from https://www.parentcenterhub.org/emotionaldisturbance/

Center for Parent Information & Resources. (2017d). *Present levels*. Retrieved from https://www.parentcenterhub.org/present-levels/

Center for Parent Information & Resources. (2017e). *Supports, modifications, and accommodations for students*. Retrieved from https://www.parentcenterhub.org/accommodations/

Center for Parent Information & Resources. (2018). *Measuring and reporting progress*. Retrieved from https://www.parentcenterhub.org/iep-progress/

Centers for Disease Control and Prevention. (2018). *Autism spectrum disorder: Data & statistics*. Retrieved from https://www.cdc.gov/ncbddd/autism/data.html

Cheatham, G. A., & Ostrosky, M. M. (2011). Whose expertise? An analysis of advice giving in early childhood parent-teacher conferences. *Journal of Research in Childhood Education, 25*(1), 24–44. DOI: 10.1080/02568543.2011.533116

Cheney, D., & Jewell, K. (2012). Positive behavior supports and students with emotional and behavioral disorders. In J. P. Bakken, F. E. Obiakor, A. F. Rotatori (ed.), *Behavioral Disorders: Practice Concerns and Students with EBD (Advances in Special Education, 23*, pp. 83–106. Bingley, West Yorkshire, England: Emerald Group Publishing Limited.

Chesser, L. (2013). 25 awesome social media tools for education. Retrieved from https://www.opencolleges.edu.au/informed/features/social-media-tools-for-education/

Christ, T., Zopluoglu, C., Monaghen, B., & Van Norman, E. (2013). Curriculum based measurement of oral reading: Multi study evaluation of schedule, duration, and dataset quality on progress monitoring outcomes. *Journal of School Psychology, 51*(1), 19–57. DOI: 10.1016/j.jsp.2012.11.001

Clark, G. M., & Patton, J. R. (2006). *Transition planning inventory* (2nd ed.). Austin, TX: ProEd.

Cohen, M. (2009). *A guide to special education advocacy: What parents, clinicians, and advocates need to know*. Philadelphia, PA: Jessica Kingsley Publishers.

Collier, M. L., Griffin, M. M., & Wei, Y. (2016). Facilitating student involvement in transition assessment: A pilot study of the student transition questionnaire. *Career Development and Transition for Exceptional Individuals, 39*(3), 175–184. DOI: 10.1177/216514341455 6746

References

Collins, L. W., & Zirkel, P. A. (2016). Functional behavior assessments and behavior intervention plans: Legal requirements and professional recommendations. *Journal of Positive Behavior Interventions, 19*(3), 180–190. DOI: 10.1177/1098300716682201

Common Core State Standards Initiative. (2018). *About the standards.* Retrieved from http://www.corestandards.org/about-the-standards/

Conley, S., Gould, J., & Levine, H. (2010). Support personnel in schools: Characteristics and importance. *Journal of Educational Administration, 48*(3), 309–326. DOI: 10.1108/09578231011041035

Cornell Law School. (n.d.). *20 U.S. Code § 1414-evaluations, eligibility determinations, individualized education programs, and educational placements.* Retrieved from https://www.law.cornell.edu/uscode/text/20/1414

Cortiella, C. (2008). *Understanding the standards-based individualized education program (IEP).* Retrieved from https://www.advocacyinstitute.org/resources/UnderstandingStandards-basedIEPs.pdf

Cortiella, C., & Horowitz, S. H. (2014). *The state of learning disabilities: Facts, Trends and emerging issues* (3rd ed.). Retrieved from https://www.ncld.org/wp-content/uploads/2014/11/2014-State-of-LD.pdf

Courtade, G., & Browder, D. (2016). *Aligning IEPs to state standards.* Verona, WI: Attainment Camp.

Curtis, R., Rabren, K., & Reilly, A. (2009). Post-school outcomes of students with disabilities: A quantitative and qualitative analysis. *Journal of Vocational Rehabilitation, 30*(1), 31–48. DOI: 10.3233/JVR-2009-0451

Darrow, A. (2016). The Every Student Succeeds Act. *General Music Today, 30*(1), 41–44. DOI: 10.1177/1048371316658327

Deary, I., Whiteman, M., Starr, J., Whalley, L., & Fox, H. (2004). The impact of childhood intelligence on later life: Following up the Scottish mental survey of 1932 and 1947. *Journal of Personality and Social Psychology, 86*(1), 130–147. DOI: 10.1037/0022-3514.86.1.130

Deason, J. (2014). *General education teachers' differentiated instruction in elementary inclusion.* Retrieved from ProQuest [Walden University].

DeBettencourt, L., & Howard, L. (2017). *The effective special education teacher: A practical guide for success.* Long Grove, IL: Waveland Press.

Dettmer, P., Thurston, L., & Dyck, N. (2004). *Consultation, collaboration and teamwork.* Boston, MA: Allyn & Bacon.

Dipaola, M., & Walther-Thomas, C. (2003). *Principals and special education: The critical role of school leaders.* Retrieved from https://eric.ed.gov/?id=ED477115

Ditrano, C. (2015). *Positive behavior interventions and supports.* Chester, NY: Dude Publishing.

Dixon, F., Yssel, N., & McConnell, J. (2014). Differentiated instruction, professional development, and teacher efficiency. *Journal for the Education of the Gifted, 37*(2), 111–127. DOI: 10.1177/0162353214529042

Dragoo, K. E. (2017). *The Individuals with Disabilities Act (IDEA), part B: Key statutory and regulatory provisions.* Retrieved from https://fas.org/sgp/crs/misc/R41833.pdf

Dynamic Measurement Group. (2016). *DIBELS Next benchmark goals and composite score.* Retrieved from https://acadiencelearning.org/papers/DIBELSNextBenchmarkGoals.pdf

Elzouki, H., Harfi, H., & Nazer, H. (2012). *Textbook of clinical pediatrics.* New York, NY: Springer.

Fan, C., & Hansmann, P. (2015). Applying generalizability theory for making quantitative RTI progress-monitoring decisions. *Assessment for Effective Intervention, 40*(4), 2015–2215. DOI: 10.1177/1534508415573299

Farrall, M., Wright, P. D., & Wright, P. W. D. (2018). *All about tests & assessments* (2nd ed.). Hartfield, VA: Harbor House Law Press.

Federal Register. (2013). *Change in terminology: "Mental retardation" to "intellectual disability."* Retrieved from https://www.federalregister.gov/documents/2013/08/01/2013-18552/change-in-terminology-mental-retardation-to-intellectual-disability

Federation for Children with Special Needs. (2013). *Frequently asked questions about annual goals.* Retrieved from https://fcsn.org/rtsc/wp-content/uploads/sites/2/2013/11/FAQs-About-Annual-Goals.pdf

Feinberg, E., Moses, P., Engiles, A., Whitehorne, A., & Peter, M. (2014). In the best interests of the child: Individualized education program (IEP) meetings when parents are in conflict. *Center for Appropriate Dispute Resolution in Special Education (CADRE).* Retrieved from https://eric.ed.gov/?id=ED555844

Fenner, D. (2013). *Advocating for English learners.* Thousand Oaks, CA: Corwin.

Fitzpatrick, B., Hawboldt, J., Doyle, D., & Genge, T. (2015). Alignment of learning objectives and assessments in therapeutics courses to foster higher-order thinking. *Pharmacy Education, 79*(1), 10. DOI: 10.5688/ajpe79110

Flanagan, D., & Alfonso, V. (2018). *Essentials of specific learning disability identification* (2nd ed.). Hoboken, NJ: John Wiley & Sons.

Florian, L. (2012). Preparing teachers to work in inclusive classrooms: Key lessons for the professional development of teacher educators from Scotland's inclusive practice project. *Journal of Teacher Education, 83*(4). Retrieved from https://www.questia.com/library/journal/1G1-300980624/preparing-teachers-to-work-in-inclusive-classrooms

Florida Department of Education. (2015). Developing quality individual education plans: A guide for instructional personnel and families (4th ed.). *Bureau of Exceptional Education and Student Services.* Retrieved from http://www.fldoe.org/core/fileparse.php/7690/urlt/0070122-qualityieps.pdf

Frey, B. (2018). *The SAGE encyclopedia of educational research, measurement, and evaluation.* Thousand Oaks, CA: Sage.

Friend, M. (2018). *Special education: Contemporary perspectives for school professionals.* Boston, MA: Pearson Education.

Friend, M., & Cook, I. H. (2013). *Interactions: Collaboration skills for school professionals* (7th ed.). Boston, MA: Allyn and Bacon.

Fuchs, L., & Vaughn, S. (2012). Responsiveness to intervention: A decade later. *Journal of Learning Disabilities, 45*(3), 195–203. DOI: 10.1177/0022219412442150

Gargiulo, R. (2016). *Introduction to special education.* Los Angeles, CA: Sage.

Gargiulo, R. & Metcalf, D. (2013). *Teaching in today's inclusive classroom: A universal design for learning.* Belmont, CA: Wadsworth.

Gargiulo, R. M., & Bouck, E. C. (2018). *Special education in contemporary society: An introduction to exceptionality.* Los Angeles, CA: Sage.

Garwood, J. D., van Loan, C. L., & Gessler Werts, M. (2018). Mindset of paraprofessionals serving students with emotional and behavioral disorders. *Intervention in School and Clinic, 53*(4), 206–211. DOI: 10.1177/1053451217712958

Giangreco, M. F., & Broer, S. M. (2007). School-based screening to determine overreliance on paraprofessionals. *Focus on Autism and Other Developmental Disabilities, 22*(3), 149–158. DOI: 10.1177/10883576070220030201

Giangreco, M. F., Doyle, M. B., & Suter, J. C. (2012). Constructively responding to requests for paraprofessionals: We keep asking the wrong questions. *Remedial and Special Education, 33*(6), 362–373. DOI: 10.1177/0741932511413472

Giangreco, M. F., Smith, C. S., & Pinckney, E. (2006). Addressing the paraprofessional dilemma in an inclusive school: A program description. *Research & Practice for Persons with Severe Disabilities, 31*(3), 215–229. DOI: 10.1177/154079690603100302

Giangreco, M. F., Suter, J. C., & Hurley, S. M. (2011). Revising personnel utilization in inclusion-oriented schools. *Journal of Special Education, 47*(2), 121–132. DOI: 10.1177/0022466911419015

Gioia, G. A., Isquith, P. K., Guy, S. C., & Kenworthy, L. (2018). *BRIEF 2: Behavior rating inventory of executive function* (2nd ed.). Retrieved from https://www.parinc.com/products/pkey/24

Gordillo, W., & Miller, A. (2017). *Progress monitoring including data collection of IEP annual goals.* Retrieved from http://www.publicconsultinggroup.com/media/1593/edu_ofcl_white_paper_pmdc-final.pdf

Gwernan-Jones, R., Moore, D. A., Garside, R., Richardson, M., Thompson-Coon, J., Rogers. M., Cooper, P., Stein, K., & Ford, T. (2015). ADHD, parent perspectives and parent-teacher relationships: Grounds for conflict. *British Journal of Special Education, 42*(3), 279–300. DOI: 10.1111/1467-8578.12087

Hall, G., Quinn, L., & Gollnick, D. (2018). *The Wiley handbook of teaching and learning.* Hoboken, NJ: John Wiley and Sons.

Hall, L. J., Grundon, G. S., & Pope, C., & Romero, A. B. (2010). Training paraprofessionals to use behavioral strategies when educating learners with autism spectrum disorders across environments. *Behavioral Interventions, 25*(1), 37–51. DOI: 10.1002/bin.294

Hall, T., Meyer, A., & Rose, D. (2012). *Universal design for learning: Practical applications.* New York, NY: Guilford Press.

Harlacher, J. E., Sanford, A., & Walker, S. N. (n.d.). *Distinguishing between tier 2 and tier 3 instruction in order to support implementation of RTI.* Retrieved from http://www.rtinetwork.org/essential/tieredinstruction/tier3/distinguishing-between-tier-2-and-tier-3-instruction-in-order-to-support-implementation-of-rti

Hart Barnett, J. E., & O'Shaughnessy, K. (2015). Enhancing collaboration between occupational therapists and early childhood educators working with children on the autism spectrum. *Early Childhood Education Journal, 43*(6), 467–472. DOI: 10.1007/s10643-015-0689-2

Hauerwas, L., Brown, R. and Scott, A. (2013). Specific learning disability and response to intervention: State level guidance. *Exceptional Children 80*(1), 101–120. DOI: 10.1177/001440291308000105

Hawken, L. S., Adolphson, S. L., MacLeod, K. S., & Schumann, J. (2009). Secondary-tier interventions and supports. In W. Sailor & G. Dunlap, *Handbook of positive behavior support,* pp. 395–420. New York, NY: Springer Science & Business Media.

Hedeen, T., Moses, P., & Peter, M. (2011). Encouraging meaningful parent/educator collaboration: A review of recent literature. *Center for Appropriate Dispute Resolution in Special Education (CADRE).* Retrieved from https://eric.ed.gov/?id=ED536983

Hehir, T., Grindal, T., & Eidelman, H. (2012). *Review of special education in the Commonwealth of Massachusetts.* Retrieved from http://www.doe.mass.edu/sped/hehir/2012-04sped.docx

Heitin, R. (2013). Advocating for children and their families within the school system: Reflections of a long-time special education advocate. *Odyssey: New Directions in Deaf Education, 14,* 44–47. Retrieved from https://eric.ed.gov/?id=EJ1018835

Hibbitts, P. (2010). 'We do this for the next child': A mother's phenomenological auto narrative inquiry into experiencing her children's school. *Dissertation Abstracts International Section A: Humanities and Social Sciences, 71,* 1152.

Holdnack, J. A. (n.d.). *Defining the role of intellectual and cognitive assessment in special education.* Retrieved from https://www.researchgate.net/publication/237760066_Defining_the_Role_of_Intellectual_and_Cognitive_Assessment_in_Special_Education

Hoover, J., & Patton, J. (2017). *IEPs for other Els and other diverse learners.* Thousand Oaks, CA: Corwin.

Horner, R. H., & Sugai, G. (2015). School-wide PBIS: An example of applied behavior analysis implemented at a scale of social importance. *Behavior Analysis in Practice, 8,* 80–85. DOI: 10.1007/s40617-015-0045-4

Hughes, C. A., & Dexter, D. D. (n.d.). *Universal screening within a response-to-intervention model.* Retrieved from http://www.rtinetwork.org/learn/research/universal-screening-within-a-rti-model

Hughes, C. A., & Dexter, D. D. (2011). Response to intervention: A research-based summary. *Theory into Practice, 50*(1), 4–11. DOI: 10.1080/00405841.534909

IDEA. (n.d.). *Sec. 300.34 related services.* Retrieved from https://sites.ed.gov/idea/regs/b/a/300.34

IDEA. (2004). *Individual with Disabilities Education Act.* Retrieved from https://sites.ed.gov/idea/

IDEA. (2007). *Section 1401 (26) (A).* Retrieved from https://sites.ed.gov/idea/statute-chapter-33/subchapter-I/1401/26/A

Idol, L., Paolucci-Whitcomb, P. & Nevin, A. (1995). The collaborative consultation model. *Journal of Educational and Psychological Consultation, 6*(4), 329–346. DOI: 10.1207/s1532768xjepc0604_3

Institute of Medicine. (1997). *Schools and health: Our Nation's Investment.* Washington, DC: National Academies Press.

Ivey, A. E., Ivey, M. B., Zalaquett, C. P., & Quirk, K. (2012). *Essentials of intentional interviewing: Counselling in a multicultural world* (2nd ed.). Belmont, CA: Cengage Learning.

Jacob, S., Decker, D., & Lugg, E. (2016). *Ethics and law for school psychologists.* Hoboken, NJ: Wiley.

Jenkins, J. R. (2007). Screening for at-risk readers in a response to intervention framework. Retrieved from https://eric.ed.gov/?id=EJ788363

Job, A. (2016). *The use of response to intervention to support struggling readers.* Retrieved from http://repository.stcloudstate.edu/ed_etds/22

Johnson-Harris, K., & Mundschenk, N. (2014). Working effectively with students with BD in a general education classroom: The case for universal design for learning. *The Clearinghouse: A Journal of Education Strategies, Issues and Ideas, 84*(4), 168–174. DOI: 10.1080/00098655.2014.897927

Kampwirth, T., & Powers, K. (2016). *Collaborative consultation in schools: Effective practices.* Boston, MA: Pearson Education.

Katsiyannis, A., Losinski, M., & Prince, A. M. T. (2012). Litigation and students with disabilities: A persistent concern. *NASSP Bulletin, 96*(1), 23–43. DOI: 10.1177/0192636511431008

Kauffman, J., Hallahan, D., & Pullen, P. (2017). *Handbook of special education.* Abingdon, UK: Routledge.

Kelly, A., & Tincani, M. (2013). Collaborative training and practice among applied behavior analysts who support individuals with autism spectrum disorder. *Education and Training in Autism and Developmental Disabilities, 48*(1), 120–131. Retrieved from https://eric.ed.gov/?id=EJ1016468

King, D., & Coughlin, P. (2016). Looking beyond RTI standard treatment approach: It's not too late to embrace the problem-solving approach. *Preventing School Failure: Alternative Education for Children and Youth, 60*(3), 244–251. DOI: 10.1080/1045988X.2015.1110110

Kirkland, E. K. B., & Bauer, S. C. (2016). Are leaders influenced by advocates in decisions on special education eligibility? *International Journal of Education Policy & Leadership, 11*(2), 1–16. Retrieved from https://files.eric.ed.gov/fulltext/EJ1138294.pdf

Klein, A. (2015). *No child left behind: An overview.* Retrieved from https://www.edweek.org/ew/section/multimedia/no-child-left-behind-overview-definition-summary.html

Knudsen, M. E., & Bethune, K. S. (2018). Manifestation determinations: An interdisciplinary guide to best practices. *Teaching Exceptional Children, 50*(3), 153–160. DOI: 10.1177/0040059917745653

Kroeger, J., & Lash, M. (2011). Asking, listening, and learning: Toward a more thorough method of inquiry in home-school relations. *Teaching & Teacher Education, 27*(2), 268–277. DOI: 10.1016/j.tate.2010.08.010

Leaders Project. (2014). *Test review: CELF-5.* Retrieved from https://www.leadersproject.org/2014/02/17/test-review-celf-5/

Leagle. (2017). *Doe v. Maher, 793 F. 2d 1470 (9th Cir. 1986).* Retrieved from https://www.leagle.com/decision/19861582795f2d78711445

Learning Disabilities Association of America. (2018). *Right to an evaluation of a child for special education services.* Retrieved from https://ldaamerica.org/advocacy/lda-position-papers/right-to-an-evaluation-of-a-child-for-special-education-services/

Lee, A. M. (2018). *Individuals with Disabilities Act (IDEA): What you need to know.* Retrieved from https://www.understood.org/en/school-learning/your-childs-rights/basics-about-childs-rights/individuals-with-disabilities-education-act-idea-what-you-need-to-know

Lemons, C., Fuchs, D., Gilbert, J., & Fuchs, L. (2014). Evidence-based practices in a changing world: Reconsidering the counterfactual in education research. *Educational Researcher, 43*(5), 242–252. DOI: 10.3102/0013189X14539189

Lewis, L., Kim, Y. A., & Bey, J. A. (2011). Teaching practices and strategies to involve inner-city parents at home and in the school. *Teaching and Teacher Education: An International Journal of Research and Studies, 27*(1), 221–234. DOI: 10.1177/0013124516658951

Lewis, M. M. (2017). Were the student's actions a manifestation of the student's disability? The need for policy change and guidance. *Education Policy Analysis Archives, 25*(50), 1–24. Retrieved from https://epaa.asu.edu/ojs/article/view/2880

Lindstrom, L., Paskey, J., Dickinson, J., Doren, B., Zane, C., & Johnson, P. (2007). Voices from the field: Recommended transition strategies for students and staff. *Journal for Vocational Special Needs Education, 29*(2), 4–15. Retrieved from https://files.eric.ed.gov/fulltext/EJ841375.pdf

Loveless, T. (2013). *Ability grouping, tracking and how schools work.* Retrieved from https://www.brookings.edu/research/ability-grouping-tracking-and-how-schools-work/

Magaldi-Dopman, D., & Conway, T. (2012). Allied forces: The working alliance for meaningful parent-educator partnerships in special education. *Journal of Special Education Apprenticeship, 1*(2), 1–15. Retrieved from https://files.eric.ed.gov/fulltext/EJ1127909.pdf

Margalit, M., Raskind, M. H., Higgins, E. L., & Russo-Netzer, P. (2010). Mothers' voices on the internet: Stress, support, and perceptions of mothers of children with learning disabilities and attention deficit/hyperactivity disorder. *Learning Disabilities: A Multidisciplinary Journal, 16*(1), 3–14. Retrieved from https://eric.ed.gov/?id=EJ874466

Massachusetts Department of Elementary and Secondary Education (2018). *Education laws and regulations.* Retrieved from http://www.doe.mass.edu/lawsregs/603cmr28.html?section=all

Massachusetts Department of Elementary and Secondary Education. (2015). *Special education surrogate parent handbook.* Retrieved from http://www.sespprogram.org/sesp/resources/handbook.pdf

Mattila, M. L., Hurtig, T., Haapsamo, H., Jussila, K., Kuusikko-Gauffin, S., Kielinen, M., . . . & Moilanen, I. (2010). Comorbid psychiatric disorders associated with Asperger syndrome/high-functioning autism: A community- and clinic-based study. *Journal of Autism and Developmental Disorders, 40*(9), 1080–1093. DOI: 10.1007/s10803-010-0958-2

McGrath, M. Z., Johns, B. H., & Mathur, S. R. (2010). Empowered or overpowered? Strategies for working effectively with paraprofessionals. *Beyond Behavior, 19*(2), 2–6. Retrieved from https://eric.ed.gov/?id=EJ885717

McIntosh, K., & Goodman, S. (2016). *Integrated multi-tiered systems of support: Blending RTI and PBIS.* New York, NY: Guilford Press.

McManis, L. (2017). *Inclusive education: What it means, proven strategies, and a case study.* Retrieved from https://education.cu-portland.edu/blog/classroom-resources/inclusive-education/

McQuarrie, L., McRae, P., & Stack-Cutler, H. (2008). *Differentiated instruction provincial research review.* Retrieved from https://www.assembly.ab.ca/lao/library/egovdocs/2008/aled/168784.pdf

MDCPS Office of Academics, Accountability & School Improvement. (2014). *Four step problem solving model.* Retrieved from http://rti.dadeschools.net/pdfs/Rtl_Guide/Ch4-four_step_problem_solving_model.pdf

Merriam-Webster. (2018). *Inform.* Retrieved from https://www.merriam-webster.com/dictionary/inform

Miller-Warren, V. (2016). Parental insights on the effects of the secondary transition planning process on the postsecondary outcomes of graduates with disabilities. *Rural Special Education Quarterly, 35*(1), 31–36. DOI: 10.1177/875687051603500105

Mngo, Z. Y., & Mngo, A. Y. (2018). Teachers perceptions of inclusion in a pilot inclusive education program: Implications for instructional leadership. *Education Research International,* Article ID 3524879, 1–16. DOI: 10.1155/2018/3524879

Montana Office of Public Instruction. (2017). *A resource guide for administrators, educators, and paraprofessionals.* Retrieved from https://opi.mt.gov/Portals/182/Page%20Files/Special%20Education/Guides/2017%20Revised%20PARA%20Resource%20Guide%20FINAL%206-6-17A.pdf?ver=2017-08-31-125132-977

Morin, A. (2018a). *7 Myths about twice-exceptional (2E) students*. Retrieved from https://www.understood.org/en/friends-feelings/empowering-your-child/building-on-strengths/7-myths-about-twice-exceptional-2e-students

Morin, A. (2018b). *At a glance: Who's on the RTI team*. Retrieved from https://www.understood.org/en/school-learning/special-services/rti/at-a-glance-whos-on-the-rti-team

Morin, A. (2018c). *Common modifications and accommodations*. Retrieved from https://www.understood.org/en/learning-attention-issues/treatments-approaches/educational-strategies/common-classroom-accommodations-and-modifications

Moyle, K. (2016). *Using data, conversations and observations for school improvement*. Retrieved from https://research.acer.edu.au/cgi/viewcontent.cgi?article=1011&context=professional_dev

Murray, M. M., Handyside, L. M., Straka, L. A., & Arton-Titus, T. V. (2013). Parent empowerment: Connecting with preservice special education teachers. *School Community Journal, 23*(1), 145–168. DOI: 10.1177/0040059918790240

National Association of School Psychologists. (2010). *Standards & Certification*. Retrieved from https://www.nasponline.org/standards-and-certification

National Autistic Society. (2018). *Professionals involved in diagnosis*. Retrieved from https://www.autism.org.uk/about/diagnosis/professionals-involved.aspx#

National Center and State Collaborative. (2015). *Standards-based individualized education programs (IEPs) for student who participate in AA-AAS*. Retrieved from http://www.ncscpartners.org/Media/Default/PDFs/Resources/NCSCBrief5.pdf

National Center for Education Statistics. (2018). *The condition of education: Children and youth with disabilities*. Retrieved from https://nces.ed.gov/programs/coe/indicator_cgg.asp

National Center for Homeless Education [NCHE]. (2015). *School help for homeless children with disabilities: Information for parents*. Retrieved from http://nche.ed.gov/downloads/briefs/idea_parents.pdf

National Center on Response to Intervention. (2010). *Essential components of RTI: A closer look at response to intervention*. Retrieved from https://rti4success.org/sites/default/files/rtiessentialcomponents_042710.pdf

National Dissemination Center for Children with Disabilities [NICHCY]. (2010). *Deafness and hearing loss*. Retrieved from https://www.parentcenterhub.org/wp-content/uploads/repo_items/fs3.pdf

National Dissemination Center for Children with Disabilities [NICHCY]. (2012). *Other health impairment*. Retrieved from http://www.parentcenterhub.org/wp-content/uploads/repo_items/fs15.pdf

National Institute of Mental Health. (n.d.). *Autism spectrum disorder*. Retrieved from https://www.nimh.nih.gov/health/topics/autism-spectrum-disorders-asd/index.shtml

National Institute on Deafness and Other Communication Disorders (2017). *Speech and language developmental milestones*. Retrieved from https://www.nidcd.nih.gov/health/speech-and-language

OECD. (2012). *Equity and quality in education: Supporting disadvantaged students and schools*. DOI: 10.1787/9789264130852-en

Oertle, K., & Trach, J. (2007). Interagency collaboration: The importance of rehabilitation professionals' involvement in transition. *Journal of Rehabilitation, 73*(3), 36–44. Retrieved from https://www.researchgate.net/publication/290075614_Interagency_collaboration_The_importance_of_rehabilitation_professionals'_involvement_in_transition

Osborne, A., & Russo, C. (2014). *Special education and the law*. Thousand Oaks, CA: Corwin.

Osgood, D. W., Foster, E. M., & Courtney, M. E. (2010). Vulnerable populations and the transition to adulthood. *The Future of Children, 20*(1), 209–229. Retrieved from http://www.centerforchildwelfare.org/kb/bppub/VulnerablePopTransition.pdf

PACER Center. (2015a). *School accommodations and modification ideas for students who receive special education services*. Retrieved from http://www.pacer.org/parent/php/PHP-c49a.pdf

PACER Center (2015b). *Training for surrogate parents*. Retrieved from http://www.pacer.org/Publications/pdfs/SP-1.pdf

Patte, M. M. (2011). Examining preservice teacher knowledge and competencies in establishing family-school partnerships. *School Community Journal, 21*(2), 143–159. Retrieved from https://eric.ed.gov/?id=EJ957131

Paul, C. A. (2016). Elementary and Secondary Education Act of 1965. *Social Welfare History Project.* Retrieved from http://socialwelfare.library.vcu.edu/programs/education/elementary-and-secondary-education-act-of-1965/

Pennell, D. P. (2013). *Designing the IEP: Measuring and reporting progress towards mastery of annual goals.* Retrieved from https://education.wm.edu/centers/ttac/resources/articles/iep/designingiepmeasuring/index.

Pierangelo, R., & Giuliani, G. (2006). *The special educators comprehensive guide to 301 diagnostic tests.* San Francisco, CA: Jossey-Bass.

Pierangelo, R., & Giuliani, G. (2007). *Understanding, developing, and writing effective IEPS.* Thousand Oaks, CA: Corwin Press.

Pierangelo, R., & Giuliani, G. (2016). *Assessment in special education: A practical approach.* London, UK: Pearson.

Positive Behavioral Interventions & Supports. (2018a). *Positive behavioral interventions and supports: OSEP technical center.* Retrieved from https://www.pbis.org

Positive Behavioral Interventions & Supports. (2018b). *What is school-wide PBIS?* Retrieved from https://www.pbis.org/school

Prater, M. (2016). *Teaching students with high incidence disabilities: Strategies for diverse classrooms.* Thousand Oaks, CA: Sage.

Prelock, P., Hutchins, T., & Glascoe, F. (2008). Speech language impairment: How to identify the most common and least diagnosed disability of childhood. *Medscape Journal of Medicine, 10*(6), 136. Retrieved from https://www.ncbi.nlm.nih.gov/pmc/articles/PMC2491683/

ProEd. (2009). *TOWL-4: Test of written language* (4th ed.). Retrieved from https://www.proedinc.com/Products/12850/towl4-test-of-written-languagefourth-edition.aspx

Project IDEAL. (2013a). *Orthopedic impairments.* Retrieved from http://www.projectidealonline.org/v/orthopedic-impairments/

Project IDEAL. (2013b). *Speech or language impairments.* Retrieved from http://www.projectidealonline.org/v/speech-language-impairments/

Project Success. (2017). *Writing standard based IEPs.* Retrieved from http://projectsuccessindiana.com/images/MKMuploads/GoalPresentation1-11-18.pdf

Rehfeldt, J. D., Clark, G. M., & Lee, S. W. (2012). The effects of using the transition planning inventory and a structured IEP process as a transition planning intervention on IEP meeting outcomes. *Remedial and Special Education, 33*(1), 48–58. DOI: 10.1177/0741932519366038

Reschly, D. (2014). Response to intervention and the identification of specific learning disabilities. *Top Language Disorders, 34*(1), 39–58. Retrieved from https://alliedhealth.ceconnection.com/files/ResponsetoInterventionandtheIdentificationofSpecificLearningDisabilities-1390487901231.pdf

Reynolds, C. R., & Kamphaus, R. W. (2015). *Behavior Assessment System for Children (BASC-3)* (3rd ed.). Retrieved from https://www.pearsonclinical.com/education/products/100001402/behavior-assessment-system-for-children-third-edition-basc-3.html

Rohrer, M., & Samson, N. (2014). *10 critical components for success in the special education classroom.* Thousand Oaks, CA: Corwin.

Rothstein, L., & Johnson, S. (2013). *Special education law.* Thousand Oaks, CA: Sage.

RTI Action Network. (n.d.). *Get started.* Retrieved from http://www.rtinetwork.org/getstarted

Ruppar, A., & Gaffney, J. (2011). Individualized education program team decisions: A preliminary study of conversations, negotiations, and power. *Research & Practice for Persons with Severe Disabilities, 36*(1–2), 11–22. DOI: 10.2511/rpsd.36.1-2.11

Russo, C., & Osborne, A. (2008). *Section 504 and ADA.* Thousand Oaks, CA: Corwin Press.

Salvia, J., Ysseldyke, J., & Witmer, S. (2013). *Assessment: In special and inclusive education.* Belmont, CA: Wadsworth Cengage Learning.

Scott, T. M., & Cooper, J. T. (2017). Functional behavior assessment and function-based intervention planning: Considering the simple logic of the process. *Beyond Behavior, 26*(3), 101–104. DOI: 10.1177/1074295617716113

Shaw, S. F., Dukes, L. L., & Madaus, J. W. (2012). Beyond compliance: Using the summary of Performance to enhance transition planning. *Teaching Exceptional Children, 44*(5), 6–12. DOI: 10.1177/004005991204400501

Sheppard, A. (2009). School attendance and attainment: Poor attenders' perceptions of schoolwork and parental involvement in their education. *British Journal of Special Education, 36*(2), 104–111. DOI: 10.1111/j.1467-8578.2009.00413.x

Shuster, B. C., Gustafson, J. R., Jenkins, A. B., Lloyd, B. P., Carter, E. W., & Bernstein, C. F. (2017). Including students with disabilities in positive behavioral interventions and supports: Experiences and perspectives of special educators. *Journal of Positive Behavior Interventions, 19*(3), 143–157. DOI: 10.1177/1098300716675734

Simonsen, B., & Myers, D. (2015). *Classwide positive behavior interventions and supports: A guide to proactive classroom management.* New York, NY: Guilford Press.

Sindelar, P., McCray, E., & Brownell, M. (2014). *Handbook of research on special education teacher preparation.* New York, NY: Routledge.

Smith, T. (2012). Evolution of research on interventions for individuals with autism spectrum disorder: Implications for behavior analysts. *The Behavior Analyst, 35*(1), 101–113. DOI: 10.1007/BF03392269

Smith, T. E., Polloway, E. A., Doughty, T. T., Patton, J. R., & Dowdy, C. A. (2015). *Teaching students with special needs in inclusive settings.* New York, NY: Pearson.

Special Education Guide. (2018). *Other health impairment.* Retrieved from https://www.specialeducationguide.com/disability-profiles/other-health-impairment/

Special Education Surrogate Parent Program [SESPP]. (2015). *Special education surrogate parent program.* Retrieved from www.sespprogram.org

Stahl, K. A. D. (2016). Response to intervention: Is the sky falling? *Reading Teacher, 69*(6), 659–663. Retrieved from https://nyuscholars.nyu.edu/en/publications/response-to-intervention-is-the-sky-falling

Stanton-Chapman, T. L., Walker, V. L., Voorhees, M. D., & Snell, M. E. (2016). The evaluation of a three-tier model of positive behavior interventions and supports for preschoolers in head start. *Remedial and Special Education, 37*(6), 333–344. DOI: 10.1177/0741932516629650

Staples, K. E., & Diliberto, J. A. (2010). Guidelines for successful parent involvement working with parents of students with disabilities. *Teaching Exceptional Children, 42*(6), 58–63. DOI: 10.1177/004005991004200607

Statfeld, J. L. (2011). *Transition Planning.* Retrieved from http://www.edlawcenter.org/assets/files/pdfs/publications/Know%20Your%20Rights%20Transition%20Planning_Revised.pdf

Stephens, T. (2015). *Encouraging positive student engagement and motivation: Tips for teachers.* Retrieved from https://www.pearsoned.com/encouraging-positive-student-engagement-and-motivation-tips-for-teachers/

Stevenson, B. S., & Fowler, C. H. (2016). Collaborative assessment for employment planning: Transition assessment and the discovery process. *Career Development and Transition For Exceptional Individuals, 39*(1), 57–62. DOI: 10.1177/2165143415619151

Stocchetti, N., & Zanier, E. (2016). Chronic impact of traumatic brain injury on outcome and quality of life: A narrative review. *Critical Care, 20*, 148. DOI: 10.1186/s13054-016-1318-1

Stockall, N. S. (2014). When an aide really becomes an aid: Providing professional development for special education paraprofessionals. *Teaching Exceptional Children, 46*(6), 197–205. DOI: 10.1177/0040059914537202

Suskie, L. (2015). *Assessing student learning: A common sense guide.* San Francisco, CA: Wiley.

Swanson, H. L., Harris, K., & Graham, S. (2013). *Handbook of learning disabilities* (2nd ed.). New York, NY: Guilford Press.

Swem, L. L. (2017). *Goss v. Lopez to today: The evolution of discipline.* Retrieved from https://cdn-files.nsba.org/s3fs-public/08.%20Goss%20v.%20Lopez%20to%20Today%20Paper.pdf

Taylor, R., & Sternberg, L. (2012). *Exceptional children: Integrating research and teaching.* Springer Science & Business Media.

Texas Education Agency. (2018). *Specifically-designed instruction: A resource for teachers.* Retrieved from https://projects.esc20.net/upload/page/0103/docs/20984-Specially%20

Designed%20Instruction-Print-Update2018.pdf

Tillery, A. D., Varjas, K., Meyers, J., & Collins, A. S. (2010). General education teachers' perceptions of behavior management and intervention strategies. *Journal of Positive Behavior Interventions, 12*(2), 86–102. DOI: 10.1177/1098300708330879

Tint, A., & Weiss, J. A. (2016). Family wellbeing of individuals with autism spectrum disorder: A scoping review. *Autism: The International Journal of Research and Practice, 20*(3), 262–275. DOI: 10.1177/1362361315580442

TN Department of Education. (n.d.). *Determining appropriate accommodations for students with disabilities.* Retrieved from https://www.tnstep.org/uploads/files/tnready_accessibility_determining_accommodations.pdf

Tomlinson, C. (2014). *The differentiated classroom: Responding to the needs of all learners.* Alexandria, VA: ASCD.

Trainor, A. A., Morningstar, M. E., & Murray, A. (2016). Characteristics of transition planning and services for students with high-incidence disabilities. *Learning Disability Quarterly, 39*(2), 113–124. DOI: 10.1177/0731948715607348

Tucker, G. C. (2018). *Differentiated instruction: What you need to know.* Retrieved from https://www.understood.org/en/learning-attention-issues/treatments-approaches/educational-strategies/differentiated-instruction-what-you-need-to-know

Turnbull, H., Huerta, N., & Stowe, M. (2009). *The individuals with disabilities education act as amended in 2004.* London, UK: Pearson.

Turse, K. A., & Albrecht, S. F. (2015). The ABCs of RTI: An introduction to the building blocks of response to intervention. *Preventing School Failure: Alternative Education for Children and Youth, 59*(2), 83–89. DOI: 10.1080/1045988X.2013.837813

University of Kansas: School of Education. (2018a). *Timeline of the Individuals with Disabilities Education Act (IDEA).* Retrieved from https://educationonline.ku.edu/community/idea-timeline

University of Kansas: School of Education. (2018b). *Advice for classroom teachers: Your students with IEPs.* Retrieved from https://educationonline.ku.edu/community/advice-for-classroom-teachers

University of Oregon, Center on Teaching and Learning. (2018). *Parent guide to DIBELS assessment.* Retrieved from https://dibels.uoregon.edu/docs/dibelsparentguide.pdf

US Department of Education (2010a). *IEPs, evaluations, and reevaluations.* Retrieved from https://sites.ed.gov/idea/files/policy_speced_guid_idea_iep-qa-2010.pdf

US Department of Education (2010b). *Thirty-five years of progress in educating children with disabilities through IDEA.* Retrieved from https://www2.ed.gov/about/offices/list/osers/idea35/history/idea-35-history.pdf

US Department of Education. (2018). *Protecting students with disabilities.* Retrieved from https://www2.ed.gov/about/offices/list/ocr/504faq.html

US Department of Education. (n.d.). *Office of Special Education and Related Services [OSERS].* Retrieved from https://www2.ed.gov/about/offices/list/osers/index.html

US Department of Labor Bureau of Labor Statistics. (2018). *Occupational outlook handbook: teacher assistants.* Retrieved from https://www.bls.gov/ooh/education-training-and-library/teacher-assistants.htm

Vanderbilt University. (2018). *What accommodations are commonly used for students with disabilities?* (pp. 4–8). Retrieved from https://iris.peabody.vanderbilt.edu/module/acc/cresource/q2/p04/#content

Vannest, K., Burke, M., Payne, T., Davis, C., & Soares, D. (2011). Electronic program monitoring of IEP goals and objectives. *Teaching Exceptional Children, 43*(5), 40–51.

Vaughn, S., Denton, C., & Fletcher, J. (2010). Why intensive interventions are necessary for students with severe reading difficulties. *Psychological School, 47*(5), 432–444. DOI: 10.1002/pits.20481

Virginia Department of Education. (2016). *Standard based individual education plans.* Retrieved http://www.doe.virginia.gov/special_ed/iep_instruct_svcs/stdsbased_iep/stds_based_iep_guidance.pdf

Walker, J. D., & Brigham, F. J. (2017). Manifestation determination decisions and students with emotional/behavioral disorders. *Journal of Emotional and Behavioral Disorders, 25*(2), 107–118. DOI: 10.1177/1063426616628819

Walton, K. M. (2016). Risk factors for behavioral and emotional difficulties in siblings of children with autism spectrum disorder. *American Journal on Intellectual and Developmental Disabilities, 121*(6), 533–549. DOI: 10.1352/1944-7558-121.6.533

Wenzel, A. (2017). *The SAGE encyclopedia of abnormal and clinical psychology, Volume 1.* Thousand Oaks, CA: Sage.

Westwood, P. (2017). *Learning disorders: A response to intervention perspective.* New York, NY: Routledge.

Whitten, E., Esteves, K., & Woodrow, A. (2009). *RTI success: Proven tools and strategies for schools and classrooms.* Minneapolis, MN: Free Spirit Publications.

Wrightslaw. (2011). *Honig v. Doe*, 484 U.S. 305 (1988). Retrieved from http://www.wrightslaw.com/law/caselaw/ussupct.honig.doe.htm

Wrightslaw. (2018). *Eligibility.* Retrieved from http://www.wrightslaw.com/info/elig.index.htm

Young, N. D. & Johnson, K. (2019). *The potency of the response to intervention framework.* N. D. Young, A. Fain, & T. A. Citro, in *Creating Compassionate Classrooms: Understanding the Continuum of Disabilities and Effective Educational Interventions*, pp. 11-22. Wilmington, DE: Vernon Press.

Zetlin, A., MacLeod, E., & Kimm, C. (2012). Beginning teacher challenges instructing students who are in foster care. *Remedial and Special Education, 33*(1), 4–13. DOI: 10.1177/0741932510362506

Zieky, M., & Perie, M. (2006). *A primer on setting cut scores on tests of educational achievement.* Retrieved from https://www.ets.org/Media

About the Authors

Nicholas D. Young, PhD, EdD, has worked in diverse educational roles for more than 30 years, serving as a teacher, counselor, principal, special education director, graduate professor, graduate program director, graduate dean, and longtime psychologist and superintendent of schools. He was named the Massachusetts Superintendent of the Year; and he completed a distinguished Fulbright program focused on the Japanese educational system through the collegiate level. Dr. Young is the recipient of numerous other honors and recognitions including the General Douglas MacArthur Award for distinguished civilian and military leadership and the Vice Admiral John T. Hayward Award for exemplary scholarship. He holds several graduate degrees including a PhD in educational administration and an EdD in educational psychology.

Dr. Young has served in the US Army and US Army Reserves combined for over 34 years; and he graduated with distinction from the US Air War College, the US Army War College, and the US Navy War College. After completing a series of senior leadership assignments in the US Army Reserves as the commanding officer of the 287th Medical Company (DS), the 405th Area Support Company (DS), the 405th Combat Support Hospital, and the 399th Combat Support Hospital, he transitioned to his current military position as a faculty instructor at the US Army War College in Carlisle, Pennsylvania. He currently holds the rank of Colonel.

Dr. Young is also a regular presenter at state, national, and international conferences; and he has written many books, book chapters, and/or articles on various topics in education, counseling, and psychology. Some of his most recent books include *Creating Compassionate Classrooms: Understanding the Continuum of Disabilities and Effective Educational Interventions* (2019); *Acceptance, Understanding, and the Moral Imperative of Pro-*

moting *Social Justice Education in the Schoolhouse* (2019); *The Empathic Teacher: Learning and Applying the Principles of Social Justice Education to the Classroom* (2019); *Educating the Experienced: Challenges and Best Practices in Adult Learning* (2019); *Securing the Schoolyard: Protocols That Promote Safety and Positive Student Behaviors* (2019); *Sounding the Alarm in the Schoolhouse: Safety, Security and Student Well-Being* (2019); *The Soul of the Schoolhouse: Cultivating Student Engagement* (2019); *Embracing and Educating the Autistic Child: Valuing Those Who Color Outside the Lines* (2019); *From Cradle to Classroom: A Guide to Special Education for Young Children* (2019); *Captivating Classrooms: Educational Strategies to Enhance Student Engagement* (2019); *Potency of the Principalship: Action-Oriented Leadership at the Heart of School Improvement* (2018); *Soothing the Soul: Pursuing a Life of Abundance Through a Practice of Gratitude* (2018); *Dog Tags to Diploma: Understanding and Addressing the Educational Needs of Veterans, Servicemembers, and Their Families* (2018); *Turbulent Times: Confronting Challenges in Emerging Adulthood* (2018); *Guardians of the Next Generation: Igniting the Passion for Quality Teaching* (2018); *Achieving Results: Maximizing Success in the Schoolhouse* (2018); *From Head to Heart: High Quality Teaching Practices in the Spotlight* (2018); *Stars in the Schoolhouse: Teaching Practices and Approaches that Make a Difference* (2018); *Making the Grade: Promoting Positive Outcomes for Students with Learning Disabilities* (2018); *Paving the Pathway for Educational Success: Effective Classroom Interventions for Students with Learning Disabilities* (2018); *Wrestling with Writing: Effective Strategies for Struggling Students* (2018); *Floundering to Fluent: Reaching and Teaching the Struggling Student* (2018); *Emotions and Education: Promoting Positive Mental Health in Students with Learning* (2018); *From Lecture Hall to Laptop: Opportunities, Challenges, and the Continuing Evolution of Virtual Learning in Higher Education* (2017); *The Power of the Professoriate: Demands, Challenges, and Opportunities in 21st Century Higher Education* (2017); *To Campus with Confidence: Supporting a Successful Transition to College for Students with Learning Disabilities* (2017); *Educational Entrepreneurship: Promoting Public-Private Partnerships for the 21st Century* (2015); *Beyond the Bedtime Story: Promoting Reading Development during the Middle School Years* (2015); *Betwixt and Between: Understanding and Meeting the Social and Emotional Developmental Needs of Students During the Middle School Transition Years* (2014); *Learning Style Perspectives: Impact Upon the Classroom* (3rd ed., 2014); and *Collapsing Educational Boundaries from Preschool to PhD: Building Bridges Across the Educational Spectrum* (2013); *Transforming Special Education Practices: A Primer for School Administrators and Policy Makers* (2012); and *Powerful Partners in Student Success: Schools, Families and Communities* (2012). He also coauthored several children's books, including the popular series *I Am Full of Possibilities. Dr. Young may be contacted directly at nyoung1191@aol.com.

Melissa A. Mumby, EdD, has worked in various levels of K–12 education for over a decade. She began her career as a high school English and drama teacher, and then transitioned into a role as a special educator, working with both middle and high school students. From there she became a special education coordinator for grades K–5, and eventually the special education director for grades K–12 at a local charter school. She is currently an educational team leader for the Springfield Public Schools, Springfield, Massachusetts. Dr. Mumby holds an undergraduate degree in English Literature from the University of Massachusetts, Amherst, as well as an MEd and EdD from American International College, both in education. Her dissertation, "Is There an App for That? Teachers' Perceptions of the Impact of Digital Tools on Literacy in the Secondary Classroom" focused on the ways in which technology can increase learning outcomes for struggling learners. She has written book chapters on strategies for helping underperforming students find success in the classroom and she is a primary author on *Educating the Experienced: Challenges and Best Practices in Adult Learning* (2019); *Embracing and Educating the Autistic Child: Valuing Those Who Color Outside the Lines* (2019). Dr. Mumby can be reached at mumbym@springfieldpublicschools.com.

Michaela F. Rice has worked in education for more than 10 years. She has worked with students preschool age through high school with various disabilities in the home, community, hospital, and school setting. Mrs. Rice holds a BA in special education, a MEd in reading and literacy, and she is a doctoral candidate in an EdD program for educational administration. She is currently a middle school special education teacher. Mrs. Rice has written several chapters on special education. She can be reached at michaelaross@gmail.com.

www.ingramcontent.com/pod-product-compliance
Lightning Source LLC
Chambersburg PA
CBHW030143240426
43672CB00005B/250